With the compliments of the Author

# Reasons

FOR

# Faith in Christianity

WITH ANSWERS TO

# Hypercriticism

BY

John McDowell Leavitt, D.D., LL.D.

NEW YORK: EATON & MAINS
CINCINNATI: JENNINGS & PYE
1900

Copyright by
EATON & MAINS,
1900.

# CONTENTS

# REASONS

FOR

# FAITH IN CHRISTIANITY

---

## I

### HYPERCRITICISM

Our age beholds scholars professing belief in Christianity who yet style Scripture a Literature and not a Revelation. Under the name of Higher Criticism they urge all that Infidelity can desire. In our own country their views have been proclaimed in a work called *The Study of Holy Scripture*. We believe that the time has come when an answer should be made, and the reasons of our faith be viewed and reasserted in the light of modern discovery and advancement.

It is difficult to distinguish the man from his system. Origen was a saint and a genius, yet he often allegorized Scripture into nonsense. Most eloquent of Latin Fathers, Tertullian, was a cynical ascetic who ended in Montanism. Ambrose of Milan, the wise bishop, the ecclesiastic statesman, the magnificent poet and preacher, said and did what our veneration wishes otherwise. Prince of theologians, peerless in argument, brilliant in style, Augustine glorified relics and encouraged invocations of saints. Immortal author of the Vulgate, Jerome was discourteous and violent. Basil, the Gregories, Chrysostom, equals of Cicero in splendor of oratory, and glowing with exalted piety, were superstitious as mediæval monks. Under the spell of that nightmare of philosophy, Gnosticism, Marcion seems to have been a Christian. No possible human errancy surprises those familiar with ecclesiastical history. During the Decian persecutions, when fire tested faith, the Clementines were read like *Pilgrim's Progress,* and after two centuries in Greek were translated by Rufinus into Latin; yet the story of the fall they ridicule as "senseless," scorn Moses, insult the Baptist, denounce Paul, and make Peter say, "In the Scripture are some true sayings and some spurious." As we estimate the past, so, with justice and charity, must we measure the author of *The Study of Holy Scripture.* We bring to the bar not the man, but his book.

Hypercriticism we distinguish from Higher Criticism. The aims and principles of the latter we approve, and it is only against an extreme that we argue. We can advance what we wish in a single proposition: HYPERCRITICISM IS A PROBABILITY, WHILE CHRISTIANITY IS A CERTITUDE.

All literary research into a far past is under a haze. Each archæologist feels his way in mist. Have we one Homer? Is the *Iliad* a unit? Who wrote the *Odyssey?* Did many minds create the im-

mortal poems? Thirty centuries have not answered
these questions. Battle is now fighting over the
tomb of Shakespeare, and his glory given to Bacon.
A hundred years have not settled the authorship of
Junius. It seemed proved that only three of the
fifteen Ignatian Epistles were genuine. After a life-
devotion to the martyr of the Colosseum, great
Lightfoot, late Bishop of Durham, extends the number to seven. Another generation may change his
estimate. Josephus ascribes the Septuagint to the
seventy at Pharos under the patronage of Ptolemy
Philadelphus. For nearly two thousand years this
statement was accepted as historic fact. The venerable verdict has been reversed by a modern tribunal. Germany and Dr. Briggs decide that the
illustrious work is of later origin, and not a trans-
lation, but a targum. Who added the Apocrypha?
Not even Hypercriticism can answer. As in Assyria so in Egypt, biblical manuscripts multiplied
differences until they became innumerable and inexplicable. Especially, puzzling and amazing in the
Septuagint its wide departures from the Hebrew.
Sometimes there is not the remotest resemblance to
the original. Hypercriticism in determining the
authorship of Genesis has drawn immense infer-
ences from the names of the Deity. In the Septuagint they appear without plan or reference to the
original. More than once in the narratives of the
creation and fall where the Hebrew has יְהֹוָה אֱלֹהִים
the Septuagint gives only ὁ εόθς. In the specifica-
tion for the ark this is reversed. The Septuagint

has *κύριος ὁ θεός* where we have but וִהֹוָה in the Hebrew.

Philo! What differences about this illustrious Alexandrian Jew! To him is attributed a writing of the first century. Then it is shown to be of the third. Again it is proved Philo was not the author. Nor yet are critics satisfied. Massebeau and Sandys maintain genuineness. Dr. Briggs dissents. The battle will be waged in the next century.

Surely we should be able to determine the period and circumstances and authorship of that most venerable of Christian symbols, the Apostles' Creed! Dr. Briggs believes that Schaff dissipated the clouds of ages. But about four years since the celebrated Harnak issued another explanation. Thus at the close of our nineteenth century the glorious old Creed is still kept oscillating in its critical suspension.

How touching and beautiful the tradition ascribing the Te Deum to Ambrose of Milan! For ages the Church believed that the sublime hymn was chanted first at the baptism of Augustine. Archbishop Usher finds two manuscripts assigning the magnificent composition to Nicetus, in A. D. 535, Bishop of Treves.

Another recent illustration is offered by the last work of the most illustrious of our archæologists, Lanciani. He and all scholars attributed the Pantheon to Agrippa in the reign of Augustus Cæsar. An inscription on the building was the ground of this universal belief, which was sustained by other pow-

erful incidental evidence. A few years since a young
French archæologist was permitted to examine the
roof of the edifice. He found inscriptions in the
reign of Hadrian more than a century after Agrippa. The walls, the foundations, and other parts of
the building were pierced in fifty places. It was
proved that for ages the whole world was mistaken.
The Pantheon is now known to have been erected
in the reign of Hadrian.

We have ourselves witnessed a revolution in the
pronunciation of the classic languages. Germany
has supplanted England. In my academic days
*Kikero* was a blunder of vulgar ignorance ridiculed
in a boy's address which was spouted daily in the
schools of our land. Now it is accepted in our col-
leges and universities. Greek and Latin are afloat.
No scholar can affirm that his reading of Homer, or
Herodotus, or Plato, or Æschylus, or Demosthe-
nes, or Cicero, or Horace, or Virgil, or Livy, or
Tacitus would not have amused and confused those
classic poets, historians, orators, and philosophers.

What shall we say of Hebrew? Uncertainties
multiply! Only within a few years have our theological seminaries grated on our ears the harsh, un-
couth, and irreverent Jaweh. Jaw! or Yaw! What
vulgar syllables in sound and suggestion! Can they
mingle in the name of the Majesty of the universe?
Characteristically, Hebrew has its accent on the ultimate, as Aramaic on the penult, and Arabic on the
antepenult. This rule gives Je-ho-*vah* instead of
Jaweh. Polish and German Jews accent the penult.

Some hold that in reading we should not accent the accented syllable. Saalschütz rejected the Masoretic vocalization and substituted the Aramaic. Amid this critical confusion we might spare our ears and compromise on Je-*ho*-vah—that most sublime name of our Creator.

Dr. Briggs would discard the Masoretic signs, and use the pointless text. With a stroke of its confident pen, young America sweeps away the traditional aids of Rabbinical learning. Left to its sure self it will "fix" the Hebrew! Yet with this certainty of conclusion these same critics are not agreed about the pronunciation of the name of their God.

Consider the exposure of our Hebrew Bible to corruption! Before the captivity the reverential care of the scribes kept the text comparatively pure. Dispersions brought dark streams of various errors like a deluge over Holy Scripture. In Babylon the very script was revolutionized. The Hebrew script was supplanted by the Aramaic script. What a flood of changes this produced! Popular for its promises and prophecies of national restoration, Isaiah would be peculiarly exposed. And even in more peril the Psalter! The worship of Israel, its translations would multiply. As the Jew passed from Hebrew to Aramaic in script and speech, while copies increased errors would grow. Writing in Babylon, Daniel composes chapters in Aramaic. Ezekiel is colored by his Assyrian environment. We have in Egypt the inexplicable addition of the Apocrypha in the Septuagint. Each book, each chapter,

almost each verse, marks the influence of exile on
the banks of the Nile. Scripture was scarcely less
exposed in Palestine. During the Maccabean persecutions the Jewish manuscripts were largely destroyed, and the corrupted Assyrian and Egyptian
parchment rolls forced into the synagogues. What
critic can prove that the Chaldeeisms of Isaiah and
the Psalter were not introduced by copyists and
translators? We are in a land of mists where certainty is unattainable. In such darkness Colenso,
Briggs, and Ingersoll have been working, and Hypercriticism now ventures to assert that there is no
ability in God himself to prevent the errors of man.

Difficulties apply to the whole Bible. Often they
are insuperable. Manuscripts in Hebrew and Greek
and cognate languages have to be searched. For
this work not ten living scholars have the aptitude
and ability; in America, perhaps, not one. Rabbins
are to be studied. The Talmud itself is a life labor.
Targums and translations are to be weighed. Quotations from Fathers open a vast field. Nor can we
overlook evidence from history and archæology.
How interminable the task! How doubtful the labor! Often how unsatisfactory the result! In the
commission which prepared our Revised Version were
two parties irreconcilably antagonistic. Differences
were fundamental, and cloud the work with doubt.
The disagreement was on the very *principles* which
were to decide the text. One set held that the combined authority of the *Codex Vaticanus* and the
*Codex Sinaiticus* should always together fix the

reading, while the other maintained that not only these two but all other authorities should be consulted. So that this division still leaves our English Bible in suspense.

We mention these facts not to oppose either General Criticism, or Textual Criticism, or Higher Criticism. Each has its wide field and noble function. Our object is to show that the man of true science is required to feel his way with conservative modesty in regions of inevitable probability. The scholar transcending his limitations we call the hypercritic. On a lofty throne he sits who decides between truth and falsehood. Presumption cannot hold with even hand the balance of eternal justice. When the Bible is involved arise questions of salvation for races and generations.

Having made these remarks, we approach with pain the critical infirmities of Dr. Briggs.

I. OUR AUTHOR EXALTS HIMSELF.

Not seldom he speaks as if his mere scholarly judgment must be conclusive. I have not counted the number of his quoted authorities, but I am quite sure that, in text and notes, he cites his own works more frequently than those of any other celebrity, ancient or modern, Greek or Latin, or German or French, or English or American.

II. OUR AUTHOR ABUSES HIS ENEMIES.

A critic must never lay aside his judicial ermine. He loses caste and influence when he descends from the dignity of the bench to the acrimony of the bar. We are amazed that a man of learning and culture, surrounded by all refining literary and religious influences, should in our age and land of courtesy so far forget himself as to call his adversaries "dogs," "evil workers," "timeservers," "traditionalists," "theological Bourbons," "narrow enthusiasts," "with obstructive methods and insincere apologies," "imposing penalties of unrighteous and illegal ecclesiastical discipline," "blind guides," "Pharisees," "Philistines."

III. OUR AUTHOR EXAGGERATES HIS OFFICE.

We have endeavored to show the nebulous region of probabilities in which the Higher Criticism is forced to work. Incertitude is its inseparable characteristic. It is the hypercritic who mistakes the genius of his vocation, and asserts that by his methods he attains results, "surely as any other department of the world's literature." How dangerous to truth when we narrow the field of proof to our own art or office! "The internal evidence," our author says, "must be decisive in all questions of Biblical Criticism," "which is the test of the certainty of knowledge—the method of its verification."

As St. Sophia was converted into a mosque, and the Bible on its walls plastered over with the Koran, when the cross was supplanted by the crescent, so Holy Scripture has been incrusted and dishonored by "traditionalists," and the Higher Criticism is to restore the immortal edifice to its pristine glory. "Scholars" of but one school are fitted for this work, and those, like the philosophers of Augustus Comte, are to constitute a supreme tribunal. We can imagine who will be the self-crowned Auriga, driving his sun-chariot with beams to wake over earth the bloom of its millennial Eden.

A Hebraist must be a specialist. He loads his memory with points and accents and paradigms, and a myriad minute things it requires a life to master. The man begins with an aptitude the reverse of logical, and his exactitude of scholarship unfits him for historic and philosophic research. Inflated he becomes amusing, unless he makes himself a blind, baffled, suicidal Samson, vainly embracing the pillars of eternal truth. In all his views the accomplished Hebraist tends to the microscopic. He is awkward with the telescope, and unfits himself for companionship with the stars. While he might piece together the pins and wheels of a clock, beyond him are the laws of the universe.

Let us apply a crucial test to our author! He says, "It may be regarded as a certain result of Higher Criticism that Moses did not write the Pentateuch." Observe! For this immense destructive conclusion, no argument! The magic word "scholarship" entombs Moses, obliterates Joshua, extinguishes Jonah, pulverizes David, bisects Isaiah, nullifies Daniel, discredits Christ, clouds his apostles, sweeps away Rabbins, overthrows Jewish national belief, contradicts the Greek and Latin and Anglican communions, and repudiates the profoundest learning of English and American Protestantism. Alford and Lightfoot and Westcott, with our Hodge and Greene and Bishop Williams, fall from their thrones before their hypercritic master.

Is criticism the sole test of authenticity and credibility? I turn to Paul! His authorship of Hebrews has been the question of centuries. Amid the conflicting authorities I wish to shape for myself an opinion. Not on *one* kind of proof, but *all!* I notice in Hebrews Grecisms peculiar to Paul. They are found in no other New Testament writer, and are not in the Septuagint. Powerful evidence! Not the whole! Our apostle's name at the beginning of the epistle, and his place of writing at the end, have no claim to inspiration, but they show an early belief in the Church. From text and tradition I rise to what with me is crowning proof. In the thirteen admitted epistles I find a masterful genius for which I know no equal in any literature. In argument our apostle is king of men. Hebrews even surpasses Romans. Of human reasoning and illustration it seems to me the ideal. No man, I believe, before Paul could write Hebrews, or after Paul could write Hebrews, and, fortified by my other proof, I conclude for myself that Paul *did* write Hebrews.

Or take Milton! In his early political and prelatical pamphlets what bitterness and meanness mingle, darkling, in the fiery flow of his eloquence! But in his *Paradise Lost* and *Areopagitica* the man is sublimated into a glory of imagery and argument which exceeds all classic poetry and oratory. Do I seek him only in a critical analysis of his text? I might as well examine the cut and color of his coat. As I can discover but one Paul, so the grasp of his intellect and the grandeur of his imagination prove there is but one Milton.

What shall we say of Moses? Above all mortals
he sits enthroned! Poet, prophet, historian, lawgiver! In his creation of genius Almighty God is
less lavish than hypercritics, and the first star he
placed in the firmament of Scripture shines indivis-
ible and inextinguishable in its supreme and solitary
glory. Whatever the species and number of its traditional sources, the master intellect of Moses pervades and unifies the Pentateuch. Now that
astronomy and geology enable us to trace worlds
from nebulæ to rotundity and organization, we can
interpret his narrative of creation and know that it
is history and not poetry, and see how inspiration
anticipates science. Paradise! The temptation!
The fall! The expulsion! The deluge! Inimitable
the touches in these historic pictures! They live in
the memory of ages, and exceed art as salvation
transcends literature! In contrast, how puerile the
idolatrous Assyrian and Egyptian legends! Moses
alone of mortals could paint the sacrificial story of
Abraham and Isaac; the career of Jacob from guile
to glory; Joseph doomed in Dothan and exalted in
Egypt; the cradle in the Nile; the plagues of Pharaoh; the cloud-guided passage through the sea; the
miracle pilgrimage in the wilderness.

One fact stands like a mountain before the nebulous deductions of Hypercriticism. For thousands
of years the Jewish nation has received the Pentateuch as the work of Moses. The supreme law of
our Republic is our Constitution. We trace its elements in England and its preparations in the col-

onies; we study the Revolution which made it possible, and the masterly discussions in the convention by which it was adopted. *The Federalist* makes us yet more intimate with its development and genius. Only as such a growth of the nation could it become the law of the nation. Let a hundred years pass! On this day let that Constitution be first presented as it now stands! It would be an unseemly and unintelligible anomaly. You might as well expect a corpse to be received as an animated body after a century in its tomb. Whatever its merits, a Constitution, proposed under such untimely conditions, would be repudiated by our nation, and hurled back into the darkness from which it came.

When Hypercriticism buries Moses it evokes from its tomb, into the light of our century, four shadows, nameless and unsubstantial as ghosts. It gives us the Judaic Code, the Ephraimitic Code, the Deuteronomic Code, and the Priest Code—sounding titles, but they and their authors unknown to history or tradition—mere phantoms of scholarly imagination. We will confine ourselves to the accounts of the tabernacle and its ministries, and to Deuteronomy. Included, we have the most minute system of laws ever given to a nation. From first to last, a series of scores of Revelations, in words, from the lips of Jehovah to the ears of Moses, and sometimes accompanied by visible and ineffable glory. Jehovah presents a model of the tabernacle with directions even for its pins. Jehovah appoints the priests, their garments, their residence, their service. "Jehovah

2

spake to Moses," is the simple and sublime introduction to these numerous personal communications. Never in our world's history have we recorded so many details for political and religious government. At the close of the pilgrimage of the venerable leader we have Deuteronomy. How does it begin? "These are the words which Moses spake to all Israel on this side of Jordan." Could there be a more distinct avowal of authorship? And it is implied or expressed in every part of the record, and wrought into its texture. As Leviticus is a communication from Jehovah to Moses, so Deuteronomy is a communication from Moses to Israel. The final message is that of a father to his people, breathing a paternal solicitude which, a thousand years after, would have showed in an imitator the icy hypocrisy of a fabrication. It directs on Ebal an altar of witness. As a witness it commands that the book be placed in the ark of the covenant. Also as a witness is composed and sung the wonderful song at the close. Prophecies, like pictures, paint the Jews as we see them this moment; and promises flash their light down through all ages and cheer life and death with words such as these: "The eternal God is thy refuge, and underneath are the everlasting arms." Here we have not only history, but a rational explanation of the genius and future of Israel. The unbelieving fathers fell in the wilderness, and for forty years Moses educated their sons into his system. After the conquest there was erected at Shiloh the tabernacle, succeeded by the temple at Jerusalem. But the nation, following the seduced Solomon, with their kings, rushed into idolatry. Bel supplanted Jehovah, the law was forgotten, the temple defiled. Hezekiah and Josiah were royal reformers and restorers. After the captivity Ezra established the worship of the new temple, and Moses came down to Christ as the author of the Pentateuch and the lawgiver of Israel.

Before we test the opposite, hypercritic view we must pause to notice a contradiction in our author. He says that the laws and institutions of the Jews, civil, religious, and domestic, were not given in the wilderness, but are "now seen to be the development of the experience of Israel during the centuries of his residence in the Holy Land. No one would think of ascribing the Constitution of the United States, and all the elaborate system of common and statute law in Great Britain and America, to the Anglo-Saxon tribes who invaded England and established the basis of the Anglo-Saxon civilization. It would be no more absurd than to ascribe the elaborate Pentateuchal codes to Israel of the Exodus." Here Hypercriticism sweeps from the Bible every revelation from Mount Sinai to Mount Pisgah. It gives the lie to each instance where it is said, "Jehovah spake to Moses." It obliterates God from his word, which it brands as falsehood. It makes the Law of Israel, not as described in the Pentateuch, a divine communication in the wilderness, but a natural evolution in Canaan, just as our Constitution was a human development. Neither Straus nor

Renan nor Ingersoll could do or say or ask more, and the subsequent admission of the theophanies only exposes the painful contradictions of a learned but illogical writer.

You will not be surprised if I now proceed to show that Hypercriticism tends to infidelity. As we have seen, it creates, instead of Moses, four authors for the Pentateuch. We will consider only two of its codes, and for our convenience call them Leviticus and Deuteronomy. These Hypercriticism ascribes to periods just before and after the Babylonish captivity. In answer to this view I will draw an illustration from Greece and America.

What gives us our confidence in Thucydides? He was a man of broad intellect, large culture, and stainless integrity. Anticipating the Peloponnesian war, before burst forth the fatal flames, he began to collect his materials. During the battles and intrigues of thirty years between the states of Greece he was a keen and faithful observer. Hence, when published, his History was received by his country as a supreme authority; and Thucydides will forever occupy the throne assigned him by his contemporaries. His History was made at the time by an author all ages trust. But let a thousand years pass! Now introduce Thucydides! All is reversed! No human mind could retain and recall such innumerable details. Every argument for credibility becomes an argument for imposture.

Our Nicolay and Hay were intimates of President Lincoln. The man and the ruler were familiar to these writers. Before their eyes passed the events of the civil war. What they saw and knew they give our nation, which receives their biography as a standard authority. Again, suppose a thousand years to pass! In this far future let the great work first appear! What a monstrous incongruity and impossibility! No memory could transmit such a vast mass of minute facts. All once in favor of the book would now be against it. Never could it obtain circulation. An indignant republic would repudiate the work as a fraud.

The principles we apply to Grecian history, and to American history, let us now apply to Mosaic history.

After the wanderings of the wilderness a thousand years pass. To the Jews Moses as a writer is unknown. Josiah is on the throne of Israel. A manuscript is brought to the king. It is Deuteronomy! The monarch examines the new parchment roll! Promises! Prophecies! A review of the wilderness! The Law rehearsed! Predictions embracing the twelve tribes! An altar commanded at Ebal! The book to be deposited in the ark! Cursings and blessings on the mountains! Jehovah's care recalled in the small matter of a camp-paddle! A song palpitating with the heart of a father! Warnings and encouragements as from Moses solemnized by death and eternity! After ten centuries no mortal memory could retain these details. Those very minutiæ which a thousand years before would have gained confidence are now so many sure marks of imposture. Josiah would be forced to condemn such a Deuteronomy as a forgery. Yet Hypercriticism would persuade us that this forgery converted the monarch, reformed the temple, revolutionized the kingdom. This forgery draws to itself the name of Moses as its writer, and is believed and accepted and venerated by the nation. This forgery is quoted three times by our Lord as Scripture in his temptation. With heaven open, and its glory on his face, Stephen, from this forgery, applies a prophecy to Christ. Twice in Romans Paul uses this forgery as an argument. All Jews receive this forgery as the work of Moses, and as such it is incorporated into the canon of Christendom.

Stronger than Deuteronomy the case of Leviticus! Add the parts of Exodus and Numbers pertaining to the tabernacle! The plan of this sacred structure was communicated by Jehovah to Moses on the mountain. Nothing could be more specific. Pins are mentioned. We have poles, bars, boards, curtains, vestments, incense, altars, lamps, oil, bread, mercy seat, feasts and fasts and offerings, and cities of refuge and of habitation—the most elaborate priesthood and ceremonial ever appointed. Details innumerable! Beyond the retentive power of mortals! To tradition impossible! Everywhere words expressing revelation! "And Jehovah spake to Moses." Presented at the time of the events, details would be a recommendation, and promote credence, while, a thousand years after, they would be a barrier, as beyond memory, and compel rejection. Hypercritic Leviticus Ezra would pronounce forgery. Yet we are to be persuaded that this forgery became the law of the new temple, and for ages shaped the belief and worship of the Jews. This forgery supplied that typical tabernacle which, under the Gospel, illustrated the sacrificial system of Christ, and in the Apocalypse was made the celestial center of the everlasting glory.

Hypercriticism thus forces us to conclude that *its* Leviticus is a forgery, *its* Deuteronomy a forgery, and, with the greatest part of *its* Exodus and Numbers also a forgery, to the small residuum will attach forgery, and the taint of the fraud will extend to Genesis, and *its* Pentateuch be a discredited falsehood. Moses a forgery! Yet Jesus Christ fulfilled this forgery, quoted this forgery, imposed this forgery as a condition of faith in himself! Speaking of Moses, he said, "But if ye believe not his writings, how shall ye believe my words?" Believe a forgery! To me such a Moses is an imaginary literary patchwork more incredible than the Koran. You might as well place Mohammed between Christ and my faith as this hypercritic Moses. But of him whose Holy Law convinces my reason and convicts my conscience and prepares me for the salvation of the Gospel I hear the Master say: "My Moses, I, the Jehovah, watched in his cradle, commanded from the bush, empowered in Egypt. My Moses I led through the sea, met on the mountain, guided through the wilderness. My Moses I inspired as a prophet, and taught as my lawgiver, and summoned to my transfiguration, and joined his name in that song to the Lamb which is the sublimest worship of my universe."

Now let us turn from the Law to the Gospel! With sorrow I make a last arraignment of Hypercriticism!

Our Bibles are full of errors. These we ascribe to copyists and translators; and it is the grand work of critical science to correct mortal mistakes and restore the text to its original purity. In this holy enterprise we have to consider Scripture as a revelation and an inspiration, whose record has not been placed beyond our human infirmities. Revelation is substance, and inspiration is form. Revelation communicates the truth which inspiration expresses. When Jehovah showed Moses the model tabernacle he could have left its description to the words of his servant. But Paul says, πᾶσα γραφὴ θεόπνευστος, all Scripture is God-breathed, and therefore an inspiration as well as a revelation. Each writer retains his individuality, and we limit the Holy Ghost by no definitions. For ourselves we cannot believe that the Holy Ghost in the same man, at the same time, in the same act, teaches truth and permits error. To admit this, for us, would make faith in the Holy Ghost impossible, and therefore veil the Scripture in eternal darkness. Hypercriticism thinks otherwise. Boldly it traces the errors of our Bibles, not only to the inability of man, but the impotency of God. "Canst thou bind the Pleiades?" Yet Hypercriticism limits our Lord, the omnipotent creator of stars, and the Holy Ghost proceeding from the Father of the Universe, and thus the Everlasting Trinity. Hear the proof in the words of our author! "The only answer is that Jesus could not give his teachings in inerrant forms; the Holy Spirit could not communicate the inerrant word to man."

We have not yet seen the full flower in the crown of the glory of Hypercriticism. This our author unfolds in a quotation to prove the importance of his science. Now we can test him, not in the haze of misty manuscripts, and corrupted texts, and nebulous regions, where scholars reign, but in an exegesis determinable by plain common sense. I will give the words our author cites and approves: "It was apparently this gift of tongues with which the disciples were endowed at Pentecost, and they spoke, therefore, not in foreign languages, but in the ecstatic, frenzied, unintelligible, spiritual speech of which Paul tells us in his First Epistle to the Corinthians."

In glowing words the Old Testament predicts the Holy Ghost. Baptism by the Holy Ghost is the grand characteristic of the Gospel. For the Holy Ghost our Lord commanded his disciples to tarry in Jerusalem. Their assemblage was glorious as the sublime occasion of the true birth of the Christian Church. On their heads fall and flame tongues of fire. They speak, how? "As the Spirit gave them utterance." They speak, our author asserts, "not in foreign languages," whereas the Scripture says,

"How hear we every man in our own tongue, wherein we were born?" They speak, what? τὰ μεγαλεῖα τοῦ θεοῦ—the wonders of God. What "wonders?" "Wonders" given in Peter's Pentecostal sermon— Christ prophecied; Christ crucified; Christ glorified. Hearing these "wonders," the proselytes were first amazed and then converted. Yet Hypercriticism makes the apostolic witnesses of our Lord unintelligible babblers! For testimony, frenzy! Instead of inspired speech, pitiable jargon! A New Testament Babel! Such is the crown of festivals in the calendar of the Universal Church! No! Hypercriticism libels Pentecost, and caricatures the Holy Ghost!

We must not forget that in Europe and America men, ambitious to pulverize the everlasting rock of the divine word, have filled the air with the dust of their own doubts. Paralysis threatens the old manly faith of prophets, apostles, and martyrs. Hypercriticism mistakes form for substance, and makes the first last and the last first. It loves to style the Bible a Literature; does it call Science a Literature? No! Why? Literature appeals to æsthetical taste proverbially fickle, while Science appeals to reason seeking by proof the fixed eternal laws of the universe. Literature is to Science an incident. If Literature is not the essential of Science, still less is it the essential of Scripture. My Bible presents itself not as a Literature, but as a Revelation, attested by prophecy and by miracle. To the Jew it was a statute from his sovereign Jehovah, Creator of the universe, guarded by temporal rewards and penalties; and to the Christian it is a redemption by Jesus, the incarnate God, predestined in eternity, with everlasting sanctions.

Amid these assaults from within and without, why is Scripture a *certitude?* My reason must be satisfied. Our quickened universal popular intelligence craves truth. For bread shall I offer a stone to appease an immortal hunger? Never! My Bible invites and dares criticism. Only these lightning-flashes of controversy can clear our spiritual atmosphere. Arius made an Athanasius, and Pelagius an Augustine. Shall my faith depend on the chameleon theories of scholars? Before I believe must I wait the turn of the spade of the archæologist, the discoveries of the hammer of the geologist, the analysis of the nebulæ of the astronomer? Must my salvation be postponed to an indefinite future? Then am I left changeful as a cloud and restless as the ocean.

Amid multiplied biblical errors insinuated by mortal infirmity I have a comfort. Differences relate to minute matters noticeable only by scholars, and do not affect one fact or truth of our salvation. In whatever language I read Scripture it is the same true and trustful guide to the life eternal. It begins with announcing Almighty God as the creator of his universe. The majesty of the Everlasting Sovereign stoops not to philosophic or metaphysic argument. My Bible is a statute of salvation proposed on condition of my repentance, faith,

and obedience, with eternal rewards and penalties.
But, with proofs to my reason! To my reason it
makes one simple and supreme appeal! And as the
proofs of Science are plain which end in laws, so
are the proofs of Revelation plain which end in
mysteries. All the proofs of my Bible center in the
resurrection of my Lord. After death did he exhibit voluntary motion? Did he see? Did he hear?
Did he talk? Did he walk? Facts these for the
eye and ear and finger! Through the visible, the
audible, the tangible, this appeal to reason! I examine in the Gospels the apostolic witnesses. In
them meet all legal tests of truth. Behind them
is ONE who compels my faith. He, in earth's history, the alone perfect man—he a model for angels
—he the moral ideal of a universe—he to imposture
impossible as the creation of his worlds—he in regard to whom the thought of lie is blasphemy—he
testifies to his own resurrection. My reason believes this infallible witness. Then, as he claimed,
he is Messiah with Godhead. The seal of his Godhead he placed on the Old Testament and pledged
his Godhead for the New. Gospels! Acts! Epistles! Each and all I can show written by apostles,
or under sanction of apostles. These apostles Christ
promised his Spirit to testify of himself. Thus behind the whole Bible is the Godhead of my Saviour.
When I examine the books in detail, all I find within
corresponds to all I find without. Evidences and
contents alike satisfy my reason. I start from the
senses in proof of the resurrection. I ascend to

Messiahship. I end in Godhead. Have I separated myself from the faith and tradition, and learning and wisdom of the past? No! Here is our English Bible! It is accepted by Christendom. Greeks and Latins are divided from Anglicans and Protestants in regard to the authority of the Apocrypha. About a thousand other things they disagree; but all the books of my English Bible are received as revelations from God by all the communions of all the world. This silent and spontaneous concurrence is more powerful and satisfactory than any formal decree of a General Council. It is the voiceless sovereignty of the Church Universal, and a prophetic sign of the future unity of a divided Christendom. With such proofs to Reason, enlightened by the Holy Spirit, the Scripture becomes a triumphant *certitude.*

## II

### UNITY

WE have outlined the argument which this work is to expand. Modern Science has discovered for us truths which are probable proofs leading upward to the crowning testimonies of Christianity. While the ladder of our investigation rests on solid earth, we hope to show that its top hides itself in heaven amid the everlasting glory, toward which mortals may climb with the assurance of ascending angels.

The first verse of the Bible declares God to be the creator of the universe. On this foundation is erected Christianity, claiming the Almighty for its author. Differing from atheism, which denies the universe to God; from polytheism, which ascribes the universe to many gods; from pantheism, which confounds the universe with God, Scripture, from first to last, affirms, as maker of the universe, a Being infinite in his nature, eternal in his existence, supreme in his perfection, and conscious in his personality. This doctrine pervades and unifies the Bible. And now physics and psychology are pointing in the same direction. They lead to the unity of the Creator by establishing inductively the unity of the creation. On this subject, striking indeed the harmony between Science and Scripture. I remark:

I. THE SAMENESS OF ITS MATERIALS PROVES THE UNITY OF THE UNIVERSE.

Early in this century Wollaston observed dark lines in the solar spectrum. How simple such a fact! Yet stupendous its results! Fraunhofer, of Munich, studied and mapped the lines. Sir John Herschel remarked that by volatilizing substances in a flame these spectral colors might show their ingredients. This timely observation Kirchhoff and Bunsen made fruitful in a method of analysis. By ingenious combinations of lenses and prisms numerous substances volatilized in flames disclosed to science their spectral lines. The same elements yielding the same lines can be detected with nice and invariable accuracy.

Turned to the heavens, the spectroscope gives its most brilliant results. The spectrum from the sun exhibits hydrogen, barium, calcium, aluminum, zinc, titanium, copper, cobalt, manganese, sodium, iron, nickel, chromium, and magnesium, while the moon and planets, shining by reflected light, indicate the same substances. Even the rays of fixed stars have been analyzed, and worlds on the confines of the universe have been forced to yield the secrets of their constitution. Aldebaran shows spectroscopic lines corresponding to sodium, bismuth, tellurium, mercury, and antimony. Sirius tells that he is composed of iron, sodium, hydrogen, and magnesium, whose flames display a brilliant white. Orion contains an orange-tinted star which exhibits sodium, magnesium, bismuth, and calcium. The spectra of the nebulæ of the heavens show bright lines like those of ignited gases. Recently in Auriga blazed forth a brilliant star, which soon began to fade, and then its place in the Milky Way became dark, perhaps forever. The beams making it visible to observers on our earth left it centuries since. Yet after hundreds of years of travel, at the rate of more than six hundred millions of miles an hour, the spectroscope discovers by the beams of that lost star sodium, calcium, and hydrogen.

Thus we prove the elements of the most distant worlds of space identical with the elements of our earth. Our universe, in all its parts and regions, is composed of the same substances.

A further deduction is inevitable. Elements combine chemically under laws and conditions which Science ascertains and tabulates. By an ingenious nomenclature their atomic proportions are exhibited to the eye. Whether the elements exist as gases, liquids, or solids depends on pressure and temperature, but in whatever state they unite in their definite and invariable relative quantities. Moreover, chemical affinities are connected with electricity, which probably controls all the subtle and infinite combinations of the material universe. On the earth and in the stars similar molecules obey similar laws. Then the chemistry of our globe is the chemistry of all the worlds of space. In our earth, in the moon, in the planets, in the sun, in the comets, in the nebulæ, in the remotest systems of creation, always and everywhere, the elements are the same, electricity is the same, chemical affinities are the same. In its vast and varied processes the universe is one in substance, force, and law.

Is the architecture of a country known from the

materials of its structures? The rocks of Egypt's eastern hills gave character to Egypt's monuments. Only the clay and bitumen of Shinar could have built Assyrian walls, temples, and palaces. The tower of Belus lifted toward the stars bricks of Mesopotamian plains. In the white marbles of the statues and edifices of Athens were expressed not only the genius but the nationality of Attic art. Parisian architecture is uniform in the color of the delicate stone from the quarries of Chantilly. Over the world each country is distinguished by the materials of its buildings. And thus with creation! In its illimitable extent it is visibly one in fact and plan by the identity of the elemental substances employed in its architecture.

II. The sameness of light proves the unity of the universe.

Place sodium in the flame of your spectroscope! You detect its characteristic lines. Turn your instrument to Aldebaran! You perceive also the lines of sodium. What do you conclude? As light is refracted from the lamp, so is light refracted from the star. Only the same law could produce the same results. Examine a dewdrop with your microscope! In that small globe glittering on your rosebush millions of minute monsters are magnified into view. Point your telescope to Sirius! You pass from the small to the great; from the insignificant to the magnificent; from a leaf on your lawn to a world near the limit of a universe. Yet here, there, everywhere the light-beam in its refrac-

tions and reflections is governed by the same laws.
The glowworm and the moon; the raindrop and the
planet; the electric flash of your street and the star
whose rays have been for ages traveling to your eye,
exhibit one universal mode of action. Thus the
light which makes earth daily visible, and the light
which sparkles nightly from the heavens, demon-
strate the unity of nature in her illimitable dominions.

But the argument is intensified if we accept the
modern undulatory theory. Newton supposed that
luminous bodies flash forth particles of their substance, which, entering the eye, give perceptions of
objects. Science now suggests a more satisfying
and wide-embracing theory. She teaches that as the
air encircling the earth by waves impinging the ear
produces sound, so a luminiferous ether pervading
the universe by waves impinging the eye produces
sight. Differences of colors are caused by differences of vibrations. As the intensity of sound increases with the amplitude of the undulations of
the atmosphere, thus the intensity of sight increases
with the amplitude of the undulations of the ether.
A body appears white when it reflects all the vibrations, black when it reflects none of the vibrations,
and red, orange, yellow, green, blue, indigo, or violet
in the solar spectrum according to the intermediate
numbers of the vibrations. And Science tabulates
in the billionths of an inch the wave-lengths of the
luminiferous ether. By its red and blue lines the
spectroscope showed the approach and recession of

light in the new star which lately flashed and faded in Auriga. Practically then modern Science accepts the theory that a luminiferous ether fills the universe, clothing it with one marvelous mantle, itself invisible, yet enfolding all, penetrating all, displaying all—at the center and the circumference of nature—disclosing the same laws, producing the same results, and revealing a single plan in the infinitude of the creation.

III. THE SAMENESS OF GRAVITATION PROVES THE UNITY OF THE UNIVERSE.

The ancients continually sought in nature a common origin and principle of all, but reached toward an ever-baffling mystery. In literary and artistic form and expression the Greeks excelled ourselves. But their philosophers became bewildered in questions about cause and force and law. What are the elements? What is the earth? What are sun and moon and planets? What are the stars, fixed in their celestial places and relations? In answers to these inquiries ancient philosophers were children. To the populace the moon was a god, the star was a god, the sun was a god. Will we believe it? Plato seems to have considered our earth sometimes an animal and sometimes a divinity. No wisdom of Chaldea, Egypt, Greece, or Rome could explain the terrestrial or the celestial phenomena. Thus in all nations, age after age, men wandered in hopeless maze, awed, puzzled, confounded before the mystery of the creation, forever speculating and forever dissatisfied, building systems only to destroy them, restless, dreaming, questioning, discussing, yet unable to penetrate the darkness of the scheme of the universe. How touching the spectacle! Humanity yearning to know and unable to know! Nature seeming to hide herself in eternal gloom! Men saw sun and moon and stars revolving about the earth which they beheld as a center. Believing their senses, they were deceived! It is not strange that the multitude parceled earth and sky into innumerable dominions assigned to special divinities, when the philosophers during centuries watched and mapped the heavens without being able to explain a single celestial movement.

Only within three hundred years has the veil been lifted. Pythagoras had a glimmer of the truth with no possible means of establishing it. Even Copernicus, who suggested the true system, had no convincing proofs. He placed the sun within the orbits of the planets, but not at their foci, so that the great luminary was supposed to be only a distributer of light without influence on motion. Assisted by the tables of Tycho Brahe, Kepler attains the truth. Yet it was by inspiration rather than evidence that he perceived that the orbits of the planets must be ellipses, and in the focus of each the sun. Soon he was led to his wonderful laws of the celestial revolutions. One thing remained. What causes these stupendous circlings of worlds? Where does the power reside and whence proceed? Is it a familiar force, or an undiscovered energy? It was the glory of Newton to answer these questions and furnish another invincible argument to establish the unity of the creation. He showed that visible about us every moment are the effects of an all-pervading force impelling the numberless globes of our immeasurable universe. Men had always seen the operations of this moving and controlling power, while ignorant of its stupendous influence over the creation. The infant dashing to the floor his toy gave proof of its existence. The boy who hurled his ball circling through the air was witness of its effects. The apple dropping from a limb was proof of its energy. Each insect, each bird, each beast, each man, each tree and twig and leaf, the sand-grain on the ocean shore, and drop within the ocean deep were subjects of its sway. Not an atom in a sunbeam, or at the center or circumference of our globe, that did not obey the force controlling the mightiest spheres of the universe. The mystery of the ages is solved in an energy known to all men at every moment of their lives, and which, acting visibly and familiarly on earth, yet operates in the moon, the planets, the comets, the sun, in all worlds at all times and in all places, binding the universe in one fellowship of existence. Each atom is related to every other atom. Each globe is related to every other globe. Each system is related to every other system. Gravitation demonstrates the unity of creation.

So far our argument has been along the path of inductive science. We now pass into a region of speculations which seem prophetic certainties.

## IV. The sameness of its systems proves the unity of the universe.

The fixed stars are suns. Some are thousands of times larger than our own orb of light and life, and so far away that their beams require centuries to reach our earth. If they shone by reflected rays they could never overcome such immeasurable distances to sparkle in our sky. Indeed, we know that they burn during cycles magazines of inexhaustible flame. But in some instances two, three, four revolve about each other. And around these as central suns must move planets, with their satellites, like our own, whose light absorbed in the darkness of infinite space is invisible even to our telescopes. Have we proved unity in molecules and unity in masses? Here we have in every part of space unity also in *systems*. These are numerous as the sands of shores, as the leaves of the forest, as the drops of clouds and of oceans. Yet, according to one common method, all the systems of worlds are wheeling and glittering over creation.

## V. The sameness of its evolution indicates the unity of the universe.

Did the ancients seek in nature one common principle? In this they obeyed an impulse of the human soul. They erred not in aim, but in method. Not deduced from facts, their conclusions made philosophy contemptible. But now Science, by induction, leads us onward to a proved unity. Her nebular hypothesis refers the universe to the same origin and development. Space is peopled with worlds, alike in elemental constitution, while differing in size, shape, density, and appearance. In our own system as we recede from the sun planets become less solid. Moving into space unestimated distances, comets are composed of thin, diffused, and often transparent matter. Also, discernible over the larger part of the heavens are spread out enormous nebulæ changing ever in size and aspect, and which seem formed of incandescent gases. Our own earth has been developed from a simpler to a more complex condition. First gaseous, then liquid, our globe is now solid. Conceive the nebulous ether rotating about an axis! It would fling off, revolving about the sun, planets, and comets, like those of our system, having the same relations, sizes, forms, densities, and motions, and indeed account for the grand geological and astronomical conditions of our globe. Hence all the worlds of the universe are conceived as emerging from the revolutions of a primitive matter visible in space as nebulæ, and believed to constitute the storehouses of systems, the magazines of the creation, and from which, according to the same laws, by the same methods and with the same results, are shaped during cycles those innumerable spheres revealed to Science by photograph and telescope. Nor is this all! What we esteem elements may be such only to our ignorance and impotence. More powerful agencies may reduce all to a single substance. This may be the luminiferous ether from whose material bosom may be evolved the universe. More! In-

capable of increase or diminution, the force of creation is now deemed one in character and invariable
in sum. The last results of Science thus make unity
the crown of creation.

VI. SEEMING REVOLUTION ABOUT ONE COMMON
CENTER INTIMATES UNITY IN THE UNIVERSE.

Certain celestial motions indicate that a star in
the constellation Hercules is a center of all systems.
Gazing thence, if this be fact, with omniscient
vision and intellect, we would behold sixty millions
of photographed suns, and perhaps billions more
undiscoverable by mortals, with their planets and
satellites; with their comets and nebulæ; with their
grace of motion and brilliance of illumination,
wheeling and gleaming and flashing about us in
sublime harmony, and showing to the eye that the
universe—one in its elements, one in its chemical
laws, one in its gravitative force, one in its evolution, one in its plan and aim—is also a proved unity
by its magnificent rotation around one mighty
world, the fit seat of the throne of the glory of an
omnipotent Creator-Monarch.

The impelling power moving so many vast globes
must be infinite. Of its personality we now raise
no question. But the unity in this illimitable creation implies unity in some infinite power and infinite
intelligence. This is the inevitable deduction from
the facts of Science. But also Scripture teaches
this precise truth. Here Science and Scripture harmonize. The unity of the force and intelligence in
Nature is the conclusion of Science, and the unity

of the Being supplying the force and intelligence is the doctrine of Scripture. Ever Scripture proclaims to Science: "The Lord our God is *one* Lord. For thus saith the Lord that created the heavens; God himself that formed the earth: I am the Lord, and *there is none else.*"

But, while Scripture and Science agree in the unity of the acting force in universal nature, they are here opposed by all religious systems underived from Christianity. Not even philosophic pantheism preserved from popular idolatry. While intellectual dreamers profess faith in an impersonal primal substance, the multitude frame gods innumerable. First they personify, and then adore, the powers of nature. Sun, moon, stars, rivers, winds, mountains, trees, birds, fishes, beasts, reptiles, lightnings, thunders—these have been divinities of men. Yet amid this universal superstition, the scorn of Science, the Bible has stood a witness for the unity of the Creator. The oneness of the Deity is the glory of Scripture.

Nor was multiplication of gods proof of intellectual inferiority. The sublime pyramids were erected by loathsome idolaters. Luxor, matchless in grandeur, shed the glory of genius over the adoration of beasts. The noblest temples of Egypt enshrined or worshiped a cat, an ox, a monkey, or a crocodile. The tower of Belus, that loftiest wonder of the ancient world, lifted its flame in honor of the Babylonian sun-god. What has ever exceeded the grandeur of the Parthenon, and the majesty of the Olympian Jupiter? The genius of Homer was consecrated to the fabled deities of Greece. Those classic nations, whose literature we imitate, whose art we envy, whose achievements we emulate, gave their treasures of wealth and soul to the magnificence of gods they created and multiplied.

Yet in protest against both the culture and the ignorance of polytheism the Scriptures, before the grand nations of antiquity, were the sole witnesses to the unity of the Deity. And now, ages after they were written, in their peculiar and fundamental doctrine, they are confirmed by modern discovery. Science aids Christianity in hurling from their temples both classic and popular gods. From earth round the circumference of the universe each triumph of inductive research thus gives confirmation to the Bible. Among deities of Babylon and Egypt and Greece and Rome and India and China nothing accords even with the grandeur of an impersonal creative force atheistic science would accept. All is contemptibly puerile and incredible. Yet the biblical descriptions surpass the conceptions of modern research. How happens this? The book of Job by more than five centuries preceded the *Iliad* of Homer. Moses wrote hundreds of years before Hesiod. The Psalms of David are older than the immortal odes of Pindar. Isaiah proclaimed the majesty of the *one* God before Æschylus and Sophocles and Euripides made the Athenian theater the pulpit of the Olympian divinities. The Proverbs and Canticles of Solomon antedated the wit and music of Horace, while the predictions of Jeremiah and Ezekiel were old when the epic of Virgil pleased Augustus and delighted Rome. In the morning of our world, before art, before literature, before science, before philosophy, majestic descriptions of Scripture are what the most cultured ages will forever admire and never approach.

Atheism now refers the universe to an impersonal and unconscious evolving force. Suppose Science should reverse this decision! Conceive that induction should establish a personal creating God! Let man reach his ideal of attainment and explain the universe! Will Science ever transcend the scope and sublimity of the sacred writers? To the triumphs of her research let her add the inspirations of the loftiest human poetry! Can she exceed eternity? Can she surpass omnipresence, omniscience, omnipotence? Can she exalt herself above the wisdom, the love, the justice, the holiness manifested to the universe in the life and death of Jesus? Forever above Science the infinite and everlasting God of Scripture! As unfolded in the Hebrew oracles, the divine nature is beyond the attainment of human capacity and the march of human progress. The descriptions of Moses, the sublimities of Isaiah, the conceptions of Paul, above all, the simple but majestic words of Christ their Master, uttered and recorded before the twilight of Science, may not only express the devotions of the Bacons and Newtons and Herschels of our world's most advanced future, but are worthy to be carried onward and upward into celestial regions, there to voice the worship of the most exalted intelligences in a glory everlasting.

Whence this wisdom residing alone in the sacred writers? Against all the idolatries of all the ages of all humanity, in language of unsurpassable power, beauty, and majesty, the Bible inculcates belief in the unity of a personal and conscious Almighty Power. And this testimony is confirmed every moment by every advance of Science! I will not say this fact alone proves Christianity. But I do affirm that it is a potent presumption in favor of the inspiration and authority of Scripture as communicated to man by God.

## III.

### PERSONALITY

EACH man is a peculiar and purposed part of this vast creation. He appears at a certain time, under certain circumstances and with certain endowments and relations which never happened before and will never occur again. As distinguished from all others he is HIMSELF. From conception to birth and onward in his development he has indelible marks which fix his personality. Mysterious property! Where does it reside? In my senses? Destroy these! I survive. In my limbs? Amputate all! I remain. Up to life's last possibility mutilate my body! I am still myself. Deprive me of reason! Frenzy my imagination, and enervate my will! Let passion and desire and affection and appetite fade or rage within! My personality has not perished. Call a man lame, or deaf, or dumb, or halt, or blind, or idiotic, or lunatic, yet while he lives the law recognizes his existence and guards his rights.

All things in the heavens and the earth combine to obliterate this personality, which survives all and defies all. I look within and without. I recall my history. I have passed from infancy, through childhood and manhood, to wrinkled and tottering age. All has changed—my form, my features, my soul. Every atom in my body has been many times renewed. Earth, sea, air, planet, sun, moon, stars— the universe has been one ceaseless transition. Yet amid these perpetual revolutions I preserve my identity with a tenacity which is indestructible.

My selfhood, then, is an indubitable fact, whose consciousness reaches to the roots of my being. It affects all my thoughts, desires, volitions, actions. It is at the basis of all my knowledge. And all in me I express by pronouns of *person*. My limbs move; my hands strike; my eyes see; my ears hear; my lips taste; my nostrils smell; my fingers grasp! How do I describe my acts? I move! I strike! I see! I hear! I taste! I smell! I grasp! Nor is it otherwise with my feelings. Love and hate and joy and grief and desire and appetite are inseparable from my personality. Similarly with my will! Nor different with my intellect! I love! I hate! I rejoice! I hunger! I thirst! I choose! I determine! I resolve! I remember! I imagine! I reason! In every possible act of my soul and my body I express myself by the pronouns of personality. From this central I radiates my being. Its recognition is a universal necessity. The language of mankind bears perpetual testimony to this consciousness in each individual of a *personal causative agency* in all that he thinks and feels and wills during each moment of his waking existence.

That philosophy is suspicious and deceptive which begins by confusing or destroying a universal and inevitable belief of the human race. Mr. Hume contradicts the testimony of Nature herself when he defines mind "to be nothing but a heap or collection of different impressions united together by different relations." And Mr. Mill concurs in this view. What! Only impressions! Selfhood eliminated! The movements of my soul united only by *"relations!"* No! my *personality* is the root of my existence. I am not a thought, but a *thinker*. I am not a feeling, but a *feeler*. I am not a will, but a *willer*. Instead of an impalpable succession of ideas, impressions, relations, I am a cause; I am an agent; I am a *person*.

And when I look out of myself into the universe my consciousness of my *selfhood* is confirmed by all I observe and experience. What mighty agencies are working about me! Yet over them, within the limits of my faculties, I exercise a control. I can overcome gravity, direct electricity, excite magnetism, command chemical affinity, nullify vegetable and animal action, and master molecules and masses. My intellect originates intelligence and my will power. I can lift matter, hurl matter, weigh matter, divide matter, and on matter impress my whole selfhood. Only in a person can I conceive this ability to reside. By a resistless analogy, from myself, to a PERSON, I ascribe the universe. But the power and intelligence in the universe are infinite. Hence infinite the Person from whom this power and intelligence proceed. My reason has brought me back to the doctrine of my Bible.

And surely, I may innocently ask, if within my limited ability to impress myself on some minute machine—if I, a point in this universe—if I am yet a conscious person—shall I say that He is not a Person who contrived and executed the plan of this illimitable creation? I know myself, and he unconscious of his existence! The Maker of all ignorant that he has made all! He who brought into being the infinite activities of an infinite universe, himself an infinite stupidity! No! Reason is expressed in the Scripture which says, "THOU, Lord, in the beginning hast laid the foundations of the earth, and the heavens are the work of *thy* hands."

The modern oracle of German philosophic pantheism, Hartmann, admits the premise of Paley, and denies his conclusion. To the Primal Substance are conceded intellect, from which proceeds *design,* and will, as the cause of *power.* But no conscious personality! Hume and Mill and Hartmann thus together eliminate God from his universe. First destroying the human personality, they exclude the divine personality. But I have found myself a conscious person. Hartmann must account not only for the thought and the force in nature, but for the consciousness and personality which I know in myself. He and Hume and Mill leave out of their philosophy this stupendous, fundamental, universal element in the soul of man. I am a *conscious person.* But an unconscious cause could not produce in me consciousness as an effect. An impersonal being could not create me a personal agent. Unconsciousness can never evolve consciousness, nor impersonality evolve personality. Admit in me a conscious and causative personality, and you must admit in the Deity a conscious and causative personality. As Physical Science brings us back to the unity of God as taught in our Bible, so Psychological

Science brings us back to the personality of God as taught in our Bible. In this fundamental truth Nature and Revelation agree. Moses knew the occult wisdom of Egypt. Opposed to its pantheism and polytheism was the race belief of the Hebrew. To the unity and personality of Jehovah he became the elected witness. By the pronouns "I" and "me" he expresses God. "I" begins the decalogue. "I" is the source of the moral law. "I" is the root of all allegiance to the Maker of the universe. "I am the Lord thy God" stands a protest against pantheism, while polytheism finds its rebuke in the words, "Thou shalt have no other gods before me." And the personal Creator of Scripture we have proved the personal Creator of Science.

Nor is our argument yet exhausted. We will now crown it by passing from abstract reasoning to concrete illustration.

Behold a planetarium! Worlds are represented by wooden balls. The sun is a globe of brass. Motion proceeds from the hand. Not a ray beams, nor a leaf unfolds, nor a fly buzzes. Repair and lubrication are daily needed.

Push out the walls of your room into the infinitudes of space! Expand the ball of brass into a sun a million of miles in diameter, throwing out from its glory light over our system; penetrating with grateful warmth the earth; vivifying grass and flower and fruit and harvest; causing air and sea and land to teem with life; revealing valley and mountain and ocean and the dome of heaven; painting with

4

gold and crimson the evening and the morning; regulating seasons; and compelling into rotation immeasurable spheres, with a motion so noiseless mortal ear never caught the sound, and a precision so exact that it is expressed by mathematical formulas! Yet according to Hartmann, the maker of the toy planetarium is a conscious person, and the maker of the solar system an unconscious and impersonal substance.

Compare a human body with the Vatican Apollo! In face and form the sun god is an ideal of grace and majesty. Yet is he cold, sterile, motionless, impassive marble. How different a human body! It grows. From an invisible germ it develops into what strength, agility, and beauty! It moves. Uniting firmness and flexibility, power and speed, ease and robustness, it exhibits the stability of the pillar with the progression of the wheel. It sees. The universe is a panorama of form and color to paint on the eye its infinitude of images. It speaks. Lip and tongue pour forth sounds to move, convince, persuade, while face and limb assist the voice as man stamps himself on man. It propagates. From one pair billions people earth. But within the body its true glory! Here dwells a spirit shrinking with sensibility, glowing with passion, teeming with thought, invincible with resolve—subduing earth and measuring heaven—while grasping after infinity and aspiring to eternity.

Yet our Hartmanns teach that the maker of the statue is a conscious personal agent, and that He is unconscious and impersonal who is the Maker of the body of man, with its hidden susceptibilities, its wonderful combinations, its exact mechanisms, its secret chemistries, and all its varied, its exquisite, its innumerable relations through its senses and organs to an illimitable universe. Humanity will rather agree with the Bible, which describes God as saying, "I am the Lord that maketh all things. I have made the earth, and created man upon it. I, even my hands, have stretched out the heavens, and all the hosts of them have I commanded."

## IV

### THE MOSAIC CREATION RECORD

To understand a writing we should study its author and its object. Moses, who composed or compiled the Pentateuch, was a descendant of Abraham, and therefore by blood an Israelite. But he was born in Egypt at her height of culture. He saw the light when the pyramids had been long looking loftily on a land covered with obelisks, tombs, temples, and palaces, attested by their ruins as monuments of noblest art. Luxor and Karnak were seen by Moses complete in their columned majesty. He lived in a country whose sculpture was grander than Greece, and whose astronomy was the rival of Chaldea. While an infant he was transplanted from a home of slaves to the palace of a king, and instructed in every branch of knowledge. During forty years he had royal and priestly privileges of learning superior to those in any other region of the globe.

Afterward he had those advantages by which seclusion and meditation ripen and mellow wisdom. In the full maturity of his powers he was suddenly translated from the court of a monarch and the society of the learned into an Arabian wilderness, where, amid mountain scenes and a primitive people, he had leisure to digest and arrange his knowledge and prepare for his future mission.

During a third space of forty years he was ruler, prophet, and leader in Israel. On him was the responsibility of saving, guiding, and training a nation. He communicated its laws, composed its songs, wrote its history, and molded its character, combining in himself abilities and preparations never surpassed. And his gifts and education were for a purpose.

The Scriptures consist of sixty-six books, and were composed at different times during a period of more than fifteen hundred years. They were intended not only for the instruction of the Jews, but for the illumination of all nations. Claiming to be the sole authoritative revelation from God of a universal religion, they aimed to supersede all other systems and make Christianity supreme over the world. Opposed to all, they waked antagonism in all. And not only are the Scriptures exposed to attack in all lands and at all times, but at all points. They assert themselves to be pure truth dictated by Almighty God. Now, the Holy Ghost cannot lie. Fatal, then, to its inspiration and authority is proved error in any original record of the Bible. It resembles a man, who, vulnerable in every part of his body, is liable always to a fatal wound. You will not wonder that a writer chosen to begin such a book was nobly endowed and carefully educated.

On reflection you will find that even the first chapter of such a work was no slight undertaking. What shall we say to the description of the creation of a universe: of its original elements with their potencies and possibilities forever; of our earth with its light and atmosphere and continents, its seas and

lakes and rivers and oceans and islands and mountains; of its varied vegetable and animal life ascending into man, of all the visible monarch; and
its illumination by sun and moon, and by innumerable stars sparkling through the solitudes of immen-
sity? No task could be more stupendous. And all
to be comprised in a few lines to circulate in every
language, among every nation, and through every
age, challenging universal opposition, assaulted
alike by science and superstition, and yet to stand
before the world triumphant in its infallible truth
and divine authority!

That I may show you more fully the magnitude
of the record of the work of the creation I will en-
deavor in a single proposition to announce its indispensable requisites.

IT MUST CONTAIN NOTHING THAT WILL NEEDLESS-
LY CONTRADICT THE PREJUDICES OF ITS OWN AGE,
AND NOTHING THAT WILL EVER CONTRADICT THE
DISCOVERIES OF ANY SUBSEQUENT AGE.

We have no reason to think that Moses in science
had advanced beyond his times. He believed the
world to be flat. In his view it was a center about
which sun and moon and stars revolved. Did he
not behold the celestial luminaries in daily and
nightly circuit around our world? He could not
discredit his eyes. All men were witnesses to the
same facts in the heavens, and generation after generation believed what they perceived. Having no
guide but his sight, Moses was constrained to accept
its testimony. Is it not, then, strange that he, think-

ing the earth to be flat, and that sun and moon and stars revolved about it, should in no single word commit himself to his own false theory, which was also received during ages in every part of the earth until within a recent period? I think that you will find it interesting to pursue further the suggestion.

To explain the difficulty encountered by Moses, and also his marvelous preservation from error, I will make two suppositions, premising what is perhaps needless, that the Ptolemaic system is that which made our earth the center round which sun and planets revolved, and that the Copernican system is that which makes the sun the center about which the earth and the other planets revolve.

I. I will suppose that in the first chapter of Genesis Moses had enunciated not the Ptolemaic but the Copernican system, which astronomers now know to be true.

What would have been the consequence? By three thousand years Moses would have anticipated the progress of the world. Asked to disbelieve their senses, men would have been confounded and disgusted. They would have exclaimed, "You declare what is proved false by our eyes. We see that the earth is not round. We see it to be motionless. We see the heavens rolling about it. Each star by night, yon sun by day, is a witness against your revelation." Nor could Moses have given an answer. To him were not known the facts and the reasonings and the deductions of our modern science. He was neither a Copernicus nor a Newton, nor could a primitive age have understood Newton or Copernicus. But I can show you yet more fully the power of the prejudice he would have stirred into the fury of a tempest.

Hear how one of the early Fathers of the Church, the learned Lactantius, raged against what is now proved to be the true theory of the solar system:

"Is there anyone so senseless as to believe that there are men whose footsteps are higher than their heads? that the crops and trees grow downward? that the rains fall upward to the earth? If you inquire of those who defend these marvelous fictions why all things do not fall into the lower part of the heaven, they reply that such is the nature of things; that heavy bodies are borne to the middle like spokes in a wheel, while light bodies, such as clouds and smoke and fire, tend from the center toward the heavens on all sides. Now, I am at a loss what to say to those who, when they have erred, steadily persevere in their folly and defend one vain thing by another."

Cosmos of Prague described the earth as a parallelogram, flat and surrounded by four seas, at whose outer edges rose gigantic inclosing walls supporting the vault of the heavens. This Bohemian ecclesiastic said that this strange mundane structure had two compartments. In one of these men live and stars move, while in the other angels push and pull the sun and planets in their celestial courses.

And around these stupendous systems of error were ranged the batteries of the Church. As late as the tenth century to assault such falsehoods imperiled life. Opposers were denounced, silenced, and suppressed. One bold skeptic was taught better by being burned. The discoveries of Copernicus, the circumnavigation of the globe by Magellan, the observations of Galileo, the calculations of Newton finally demonstrated the rotundity and revolution of the earth, and the world and the Church were persuaded of a truth whose belief had made martyrs.

Now, if such bitter opposition existed as late as the sixteenth century; if the purest and most gifted resented what seemed to contradict their senses; if flames were argument against the facts and laws of nature, how revolting and impossible would the Copernican system have appeared to Chaldean and Egyptian astronomers in the times of Moses! How much more hateful to the superstitious multitude! Premature revelation would have made obstacles to faith which were both unnecessary and insuperable. There was a divine wisdom in not anticipating the true system of the universe. It was better for our race to learn the laws of geology and astronomy by toilsome but educating centuries of induction and enterprise than to be puzzled and bewildered by communications at once unintelligible and unnecessary to that salvation which is the grand purpose of the Bible.

II. I will now suppose that the first chapter of Genesis had recorded not the Copernican but the Ptolemaic system.

For thirty centuries the world would have rested in the error. A few might have doubted. Occasionally would have come faint suggestions that the sun and not the earth was the center of our system. Pythagoras before our era, in the fifth century Capella, and in the fifteenth De Cusa, had glimpses of the truth, which were prophecies of a coming splendor of discovery. At Thorn, in Prussia, in 1473, Copernicus was born. He received his doctor's degree at Cracow, studied astronomy at Bologna, taught at Rome, and became a canon at Frauenburg. A thought in his soul became a living fire. Sun and planets, he believed, do not revolve about the earth, but earth and planets do revolve about the sun. He risked life by the publication of his opinions. On his deathbed he first saw his book on *The Revolution of the Heavenly Bodies.* A look, and his eyes close forever! His grave saves him from his enemies. The man they bury, but not his doctrine. It survives in his book. All the ecclesiastical batteries thunder against it, although it is the eternal truth of God. Priests draw arguments from Aristotle, Aquinas, and Scripture to prove that the earth is the center of the system. If Protestants do not burn the believers in Copernicus, they denounce his doctrine as absurd and subversive of the faith. Luther, author of the Reformation, foe to popes, hero and herald of the spiritual and intellectual emancipation of humanity, bursts forth:

"People gave ear to an upstart astrologer, who strove to show that the earth revolves, and not the heavens, or the firmament, the sun, and the moon."

But what of the conservative Melanchthon? He was the theologian of the Reformation, mild and meditative, who often allayed storms and harmonized antagonisms. Yet against Copernicus he was more violent than the impetuous Luther himself. Mark his contemptuous words:

"The eyes are witnesses that the heavens revolve in the space of twenty-four hours. But certain men, either from love of novelty or to make display, have concluded that the earth moves, and they maintain that neither the eighth sphere nor the sun revolves. It is a want of honesty and decency to assert such notions publicly, and the example is pernicious."

Bruno was another advocate of the new system. On him fell the storm from which the grave protected Copernicus. Pursued from country to country, Bruno was arrested, imprisoned, and burned. His ashes were scattered to the winds of heaven, testifying as they flew to the hatred against that grand doctrine now the center of all astronomical science.

Not long after Galileo perfected his telescope. Tauntingly the foes of Copernicus had urged, "If your doctrine be true, Venus would show phases like the moon." "You are right," said the great Florentine; "I know not what to answer. God is good, and will in time find answer to this objection." How touching such candor! How beautiful such faith! How magnificent its reward! See Galileo with his telescope. He points it to the heavens. It is on Venus. What amazement and triumph on the face of the astronomer! God's time has indeed come. Galileo beholds proof of the Copernican doctrine. The veil of ages is lifted. A spectacle of beauty is disclosed before invisible to man. Seen through the telescope Venus no longer sparkles in starlike splendors. Her golden crescent shines on the deep blue of heaven. Sight confirms reason. The telescope of Galileo verifies the truth of Copernicus. Corrected now the testimony of the eye, and proved the great central fact of the system and our universe!

But the battle was not over. It only began with that first vision of the glory of Venus. Ecclesiastical thunders burst over the astronomer. He is accused as a heretic. He is pronounced in league with Satan. He is guilty of infernal error. In Italy, in Germany, in Holland, in France the great universities condemn the doctrine of Copernicus and the discovery of Galileo. Church and world rage against the everlasting truth of creation. Still Galileo turns his telescopic eye to the heavens. Fresh wonders reveal themselves through sense to his intellect. He points his instrument to the moon and sees on her bright face her valleys and her mountains. On the sun he discovers spots. Tempests on earth burst into fresh fury with every revelation from the sky. Hell strives to quench the celestial light of truth. The Copernican theory is condemned in the following memorable words:

"The first proposition, that the sun is the center and does not revolve about the earth, is foolish, ab-

surd, false in theology, and heretical because ex-
pressly contrary to Scripture; and the second proposition, that the earth is not the center, but revolves
about the sun, is absurd, false in philosophy, and
from a theological point of view, at least, opposed
to the true faith."

Galileo also is commanded "to abstain from sus-
taining, teaching, or defending that opinion in any
manner whatever."

Nor have we reached the saddest act of the tragic
history. Unequal to martyrdom, the illustrious astronomer escapes by abjuration the doom of fire.
No humiliation was ever more pitiable or more
touching. Fear by falsehood escapes torture. Hear
the sworn lie of genius extorted by ignorant tyr-
anny:

"I, Galileo, being in my seventieth year and a
prisoner, and on my knees, having before my eyes
the Holy Gospels, which I touch with my hands,
abjure, curse, and detest the error and the heresy
of the movement of the earth."

Surely such a degradation will appease ecclesiastic fury! No! Brought from prison Galileo was
deprived of his position, separated from his family,
exiled from his friends, until old and blind and
wasted and miserable he died overcome by disease
and sorrow. He was buried, not among his rela-
tives, nor with ceremonies suitable to his genius and
discoveries, but borne to a solitary grave, and for a
century left without epitaph or monument.

But against rage and envy and ignorance truth

prevailed. Reason by the telescope compelled the eye to reverse its testimony, and dispelled the shadows of the centuries. The Copernican system is accepted with the assurance of a mathematical axiom. A schoolboy would scorn to doubt it, and it has become part of the popular belief of our civilized humanity.

The fierce conflicts described show how deeply the Ptolemaic system was rooted among mankind, and how hard to dislodge from the soul what seemed proved by the eye. As appearances testified, Moses thought that sun and star revolved about the earth. Yet in describing the creation of the universe his own opinions make no part of his record. Why did he not write what he believed? Men publish their convictions. Does not this absence of the private errors of Moses from his history raise a powerful presumption of his inspiration? It leads us to believe that he was under the guidance of the Eternal Spirit of Truth.

But let us return to our supposition. Suppose the Ptolemaic system had been wrought into our Bibles! For ages its errors would have been undetected. At last, however, the veil would have been lifted from the antiquated lie, and the Scripture exposed to the scorn of its triumphant enemies. Copernicus was a Christian. Kepler was a Christian. Galileo was a Christian. Newton was a Christian. How would the faith of those good and grand men have been shocked and shattered had the error of Ptolemy been part of the record of Moses! There can be no answer where the Book of Nature is opposed to the Book of Revelation.

You will now, I think, agree with me that the Mosaic history of the creation evinced a superhuman wisdom in not needlessly contradicting the prejudices of the world for three thousand years by prematurely announcing the Copernican system, and that only the same superhuman wisdom could have kept out of his record the belief of the narrator in the Ptolemaic system. It is certainly astonishing that a narrative should be so constructed that without the slightest contortion it should be equally suitable to a time of knowledge and a time of ignorance; should keep its place during centuries of astronomical error, and defy assault during centuries of astronomical truth; and should in an age of darkness on every subject of science lay the foundations of a universal religion which endures the scrutiny of an age of unexampled light.

Nor will our regard for the Mosaic narrative be diminished when we compare it with the Chaldean account procured and deciphered by the late Mr. George Smith. Amid piles of broken cuneiform tablets and cylinders in the British Museum that gentleman noticed some characters which seemed to describe the deluge, and visited the Orient in search of missing fragments. His sagacity and energy were rewarded. Amid the ruins of Koyunjik he found the wanted tablets. He also discovered cuneiform records of the creation. Exposed for ages to the elements, and scattered by wild Arabs, cylinders of clay, after centuries of separation, have been brought together and enable us to contrast puerile Chaldean records with the sublime Hebrew Scriptures.

In opposition to the unity of creation as proved by modern Science we perceive polytheism in the recovered fragments. Chaos is a goddess producing inferior deities. We have the names of the chief divinities in the Assyrian Pantheon. Tiamat is universal mother. And there are the god Sar, the god Kisar, the god Anu, the god Assur, the god Bel, the god Hea, the god Niku, and the god Nin-siku. Uri, the moon, is a god, and Shamas, the sun, is a god. Imagine Science reconciling such childish inventions with her grand discoveries! Accepting the Chaldean record, our modern astronomer would through his telescope study sun and moon as a pair of gods, and our steamships would be plowing the bosom of our divine and adorable mother Tiamat.

How puerile, too, the thought and style of the Assyrian fables! What addition do they make to human knowledge? Can they stimulate intellect? Are they not whimsical traditions of an infantine idolatry? They seem polytheistic corruptions of the biblical original, which shines with new beauty and splendor in contrast with this dim and defaced copy. In the comparison we realize how simple, how sublime, how majestic the Mosaic narration. How it intertwines itself with history, art, and literature! It challenges science, and awakes investigation. In its exposition it accumulates around itself all the

treasures of all the ages of all the earth whose creation it so grandly and worthily describes. The first
chapter of Genesis is a suitable introduction for a
religion claiming to be founded on the cross of a
divine Saviour, to be thus touched with the glory
of Godhead, to be a preparative for the solemnities
of judgment and the rewards of a life everlasting.

5

## V

### PROTOPLASM

BEFORE the world are two theories of the origin of man. One asserts that he was evolved from protoplasm, and the other affirms that he was created by Almighty God. We propose to examine which view is more agreeable to reason.

The second chapter of Genesis seems an historical relation. If a myth, the Bible is a myth. The formation of Adam is related as a fact, as the birth of Christ is related as a fact. You can no more esteem it a fiction than you can call imaginary each history and biography in the Old and in the New Testament. Jehovah forms a body from dust. Jehovah breathes life into the dead organism. Jehovah from sleeping Adam takes a rib and shapes a woman. From this pair, lords of earth, tempted, disobedient, and cursed, yet redeemed, spring the billions who people time and eternity. Only the fall of Adam makes possible the salvation of Christ. Without sin, no atonement, no remission, no regeneration, and after death neither resurrection, nor judgment, nor eternal award. Convert into myth the narration of the transgression in paradise, and you destroy the very foundation of redemption. Paul is the great interpreter of Scripture. Sin and death he traces to Adam as atonement and resurrection to Christ. With him, the fall is a truth surely as the death on the cross is a truth. And in all ages this has been the view of the Universal Church.

Instructors in seminary and pulpit have adopted an opposite theory—evolution. This supposes the lowest possible organism, resembling the amœba or jellyfish, and denominated protoplasm. From it develops all our world-life. Each higher vegetable and animal species evolves from a lower until man is attained, who consummates an ascent during cycles inconceivable in duration.

Science confronts us with a universal and invariable fact for which philosophy supplies a reason. From an animalcule in a drop, through billions of gradations in sea, air, and earth, rising to the whale, the condor, the elephant, and man, we find innumerable species separated by impassable barriers. Beyond a certain limit they never propagate. Nature has defied and defeated Science in every attempt to produce life except from animate organism, and to demolish distinctions between vegetable and animal forms. Go back cycles in geological eras! Pierce the oldest fossilized rocks! Examine them with microscopic care! Mastodons and crustacea obey the same law. In the twilight of the minutest organized existence species are as sharply divided as in the highest developments of our times. There is no appreciable tendency toward confusion. Well for man that his petty efforts to intermingle have been baffled! His success would fill earth with transitional monsters whose loathsome aspects would make his life horrible, and whose fierce dispositions might make it impossible. In nothing do love and wisdom more appear than in the eternal decree against the perpetuation of hybrids. Yet, were evolution true, transitional forms would be everywhere visible with universal disorder and destruction. Mr. Darwin admitted the force of this unanswerable objection, and has given the best refutation of his own theory. He says:

"Why is not every geological formation and every stratum full of such intermediate links? Geology does not certainly reveal any such finely graduated organic chain, and this is, perhaps, the most obvious and serious objection that can be urged against the theory. The explanation, I believe, lies in the *extreme imperfection of the geological record.*"

All the billions of billions of billions of instances of animal and vegetable propagation during cycles are against the Darwinian theory of evolution, and yet that theory is to be accepted on the supposition that if we had more facts, it might be true. The theory, then, is not proved by facts, but facts are presumed to meet the theory. By such a procedure we overthrow every principle of induction on which rests the whole structure of Modern Science.

We return to protoplasm. It is matter. How can matter evolve mind? Can length, breadth, thickness, weight, give birth to thought and feeling and volition? From the unperceiving clod to the sentient soul, does not the transition seem impossible? Certainly, unless you ascribe intellection to the brain itself! Then you must believe that matter thinks, matter feels, matter wills, matter writes poems, and makes statues, and masters sciences, and knows and does its duty, and aspires to worship and immortality. Here again the common sense of mankind is with Scripture and against protoplasm. The very language of humanity testifies to its belief in the eternal difference between matter and spirit.

Evolution begins with taking for granted protoplasm. Whence protoplasm? Protoplasm is a fiction. It has no place in Science as a fact. Cause must be adequate to effect. The tree is included in its seed. The bird is included in its egg. The light is included in the sun. Given seed, egg, sun, then tree and bird and light follow as effect from cause. So, if the universe was developed from protoplasm, it was contained in protoplasm. Where is the scientific proof? This is impossible. Evolution takes for granted the universe for which it would account. Or would it go back for the origin of our race to the nebulæ of the heavens? I can as easily conceive that man comes from earth-dust as sky-mist.

In the temple of Diana at Ephesus was a statue of the goddess reputed to have fallen from the skies. Perhaps the priests knew better, but the populace believed in the image. On its breast were the symbols of maternity, and it was worshiped as the mother of all. While this was the faith of the multitude, the ancient philosophers taught that Nature herself was divine, in ceaseless change, and even producing our world as a deity. We have, therefore, four theories which we can place in contrast, and for ourselves judge which is most probable:

From pantheism we have, God is the universe; from Diana's statue, a universe; from protoplasm, a universe; from Almighty God, a universe.

Matter from spirit! The visible from the invisible! The ponderable from the imponderable! The tangible from the intangible! This is in its *mode* a mystery, but not, like the three other beliefs, an absurdity. And we have in ourselves an analogy.

Thought alone excites thought. Not words, or color, or marble stimulate thought. They are powerless except as interpreters of thought. A rough stone does not awaken the soul. Carve it into a statue! It kindles in you an intellectual glow. Mountain rocks you pass without a thrill. Build them into a temple! Your emotions are sublime. Not the shapeless iron, but the contrived machine stirs your admiration. When the solitary wilderness is converted into the populous city you burst into amazement. In each instance, in proportion to the power of the originating thought is the power of the exciting thought.

Turn from art to Nature! How does she affect us? As nothing else she quickens and expands. Tame and poor our impressions from our human works compared with our impressions from the universe. Does thought alone stimulate thought? Then it is the thoughts in nature that stir the thoughts in our souls.

But with the thought is force; and always the thought directs the force. Thought and force are inseparable, and both partake the unity and infinity

of nature—that is, the universe has its key in Power
and Intelligence. What is their source? Not the
molecules of matter. These move, indeed, but as
they are moved by electricity, by magnetism, by
gravity, by chemical attraction, by vegetable and
animal energy. But plainly blind forces do not orig-
inate a Power and Intelligence which they obey.
I ask for their author, and say for myself that the
most rational answer to my question is not in pantheism, nor idolatry, nor protoplasm, but in the
Everlasting, the Omniscient and Omnipresent and
Personal Spirit represented in my Bible as the cause
of the universe.

# VI

## CREATION MYSTERIES

How impressive the progressive glories of the creation! Lavished over the universe are the infinite proofs of an exquisite benevolent and comprehensive wisdom. All this is included in the Mosaic record. Then on its fair page we are met by a blot. Shall the Maker mar his work? Sin! Pain! Death! Are these specters to be let loose against man? We are astounded by a curse that withers paradise, blasts our world, and makes mortal our race. Our Bible informs us that Jehovah pronounced the fearful and universal doom which he executed. Jehovah by oceans swept millions into eternity. Jehovah plagued Egypt and engulfed her army. Jehovah decreed that a generation should perish in the wilderness, commanded the extermination of Canaanites, commissioned Babylonians, Ninevites, and Egyptians to scourge Israel by fire and sword, and then hurled to ruin the executors of his own judgments. Jews crucified Christ. For this crime Romans burned their temple and destroyed their cities, and then were themselves given over to Goth, Hun, and Vandal. Ever since history has been a record of war. But God directs history. So our Bibles teach. God rules; God exalts; God depresses; God punishes; God rewards. Nothing is left to chance. All is one everlasting plan. Unanchored in Divine Sovereignty man is a waif in the universe.

It is not wonderful that we are bewildered by such representations claiming to be inspired truth. Yet I think I can show that our perplexity is not in the Bible, nor from the Bible, but *behind* the Bible. It is in NATURE. Questions from nature are more unanswerable than questions from Scripture. Let us then turn to nature!

I will illustrate my position first by a *shark*. He is the locomotive of the deep, outspeeding steamships. Compound engines are dwarfed before the perfection of his propulsive power, and compared with his fin and tail twin-screws are clumsy contrivances. He is said to make a hundred miles an hour, and could be at Queenstown while our ocean racers are yet whistling in the fog banks. What feeds the shark's muscle to give him speed? Not coal, but life. He exists on fishes. Death impels his fin and tail. His jaw and teeth and maw were made to kill and devour. Because of his anatomy and his fierceness he swims king of the deep. What pangs he inflicts on the beautiful creatures sporting along his ocean pathway! Yet God made them for each other. And through those illimitable waters prevails the same law. A whale swallows billions of small fishes. By his horrid arms the devilfish clasps his victims, and kills as much by terror as by pressure. All the smaller fishes prey on each other. Science shows that they were made to do so. Crab and lobster and their monstrous fellows were formed to exist by devouring. Ocean is one planned world of death. Its waters are tinged with blood. Daily hecatombs of its suffering creatures are sacrificed to the grim necessities of appetite.

Nor is air more merciful. On your wood path see that little bunch of feathers! What does it tell you? That a hawk pounced on a songster of the grove, and you behold all that is left of the ecstatic creature whose melody thrilled you in the morning. Swooping from his cloud the eagle bears in his talons the dove aloft to yon solitary mountain nest, where an unfledged brood clamor for blood. Birds live on birds. Insects devour insects. All winged creatures feed on other winged creatures. This air which folds round our world with life is one boundless scene of death.

Earth is no exception to the plan visible in sea and air. The lion eats the lamb. Tigers prowl to kill. Panthers and leopards catch and slay and gorge. Large animals live on small animals. Nor by accident! Examine the lion's jaw! Observe his claws and teeth! Study his whole system! He must have flesh and blood for health. In his maw is a fierce life-hunger. The law of his being impels him to slay and eat. And so over earth! Even the animalculæ in a glittering dewdrop are whirling about bent madly on devouring their microscopic fellows. Each globe on your rosebush sparkling so gayly to the morning sun is a slaughterhouse.

What of man? For food and sport he kills millions. Our race would degenerate if it ceased to slay. Man's constitution craves and requires flesh. He cannot help killing. Furs and feathers for his comfort and fashion imply death. Except by pain he cannot enjoy his bed of down. What grim necessities are hidden in his abattoir! We avert our eyes and ears, but unpleasant suggestions come from those bleating and bellowing creatures meekly protesting against anticipated slaughter. Always in our cities are running streams of blood. Over our country it is a daily river. A red annual ocean over our world! Ax! knife! bullet! What a ghastly apparatus supplies our tables! We partake insensible to the agonies involved in our wants and pleasures.

Our terrestrial constitution is one of pain. You and I would never have ordained such a scheme of woe and death. Yet God made it. From first to last he is contriver. Many indeed are the marks of loving wisdom. The lamb frisks in the field. The bird trills the air with joy. The goldfish glides round happy in his globe prison. Insects dart about in seeming ecstasy. Man has innumerable springs and hours of pleasure. When the air is filled with sunbeams; when the ocean throbs in the morning light; when the earth is glad with the songs and blossoms and fragrances of spring, it is hard to realize that each realm is an abode of death, and conceals beneath its beauty ghastly scenes of pain. Yet while the lark carols the hawk strikes. While the salmon sports the shark seizes. While the deer frisks the man slays. Vegetables grow out of soils enriched by death. Earth is filled with graves and ocean peopled by skeletons. Amid sights and sounds of beauty and of joy rises one universal wail of pain. Humanity stands dumb before the mystery of its own constitution. Millions of years prior to man our world was the same. Rocks from dim preadamite ages, bristling with teeth and claws and every preparation for battle, defense, and carnage, bear testimony to monsters of land and sea and air vaster and fiercer than the most formidable of our modern era. During cycles has been waged this war of races compelled by natures created by the Almighty Sovereign of the universe.

From nature we will turn to Providence! How terrible the inexplicable severity of events! An architect's miscalculation wrecks a building, and wounds and maims and kills a multitude who had no part in the mistake. On a locomotive an engineer misinterprets a signal. To sleeping and confiding passengers comes the catastrophe amid agonies of fire and death. The captain's error sinks his ship, and sends down into the dark abysses of the ocean victims of another's incapacity. A commander's blunder loses an army, blights a kingdom, and imperils liberty herself. Crimes of a despot fill an empire with blood and horror, involving good and bad, like an earthquake, a famine, or a pestilence. Over our humanity is this doom. Its moral disorders baffle reason. Life's rewards go often to the least deserving. During ages evil will seem to triumph over good. Strong nations grind weak tribes out of existence. Tyrannies conquer and prosper. Neroes behead Pauls. Popes burn saints. Inquisitors kill millions and enrich themselves with the murder of innocence. Virtue in rags, blind and lame and starving at the gate with dogs, while vice impurpled in her palace, is crowned with splendor and feasting in luxury! The cry of wrong ever piercing heaven!

Each man seeks a solution of these mortal problems. Many explanations have been attempted. The ancient Persian told us that there was a spirit of light and a spirit of darkness in everlasting war. Gnostics traced the ills of the world to an ineradicable evil in matter. Pantheism teaches that we are evolved from the universe and dissolved into the universe in cycles of eternal change. Buddhism seeks relief in submission, and Brahmanism in expiation. Stoicism took refuge in the dignity of philosophy, and Epicureanism in the oblivion of pleasure. Atheism denies everything, scorns everything, mocks and ridicules everything. Our modern agnosticism folds its arms and admits inevitable and inconquerable ignorance. But in all these systems is a confession of difficulties for which they afford humanity no rational and sufficient relief. The end of each is despair. If nothing better can be offered, then in life's great woes suicide is wisdom.

All these inexplicable moral difficulties are in nature, and would have existed had there never been a Bible, and would remain if the Bible were obliterated. Indeed, nature is a greater puzzle than the Bible. For innumerable sufferings in nature I can find no reason, while in the terrible inflictions of the

Bible I perceive a justice. In animal pangs I see
no moral end—in plagues sent on men and nations
is a plain punitive and disciplinary purpose. Adam
sinned and was cursed. The world sinned and was
deluged. Egypt sinned and was scourged. See
Sinai! Its top flashes flames. Cloud and glory are
there together. Amid mingling darkness and splendor Jehovah talks with Moses and on the summit
of the mountain writes in stone commandments
against idolatry, while at the base the people are
worshiping a calf of gold. Israel sinned and perished. Canaanites sinned and were exterminated.
Jews sinned and were exiled. Babylonians and Ninevites and Egyptians sinned and were blasted. Rome
sinned and fell. Humanity sins and suffers. So
teaches our Bible, and in the inflictions of Jehovah
on men and nations we perceive a justice. But the
dove does not sin. The lamb does not sin. The
goldfish does not sin. In air, land, and sea innumerable beings do not sin. Yet they thrill the world
with pain and shadow it with death. You perceive
that the difficulties in nature exceed the difficulties
in the Bible. In the Bible I see a justice, and in
nature I see no justice. Over the animal world is
one impenetrable cloud. In this universal pain of
creatures without moral agency or responsibility I
can discover no right, no love, no wisdom. Let our
infidels then quarrel with nature! Having first explained nature, they may assault the Bible. Creation,
not Revelation, is their battlefield.

Now, for an adjustment of every seeming injustice

in this world Christianity refers us to the next.
Against the distribution of rewards and punishments
in our present life humanity protests. By one common resistless instinct our race looks for relief and
reconcilement to eternity. And for this moral yearning in man the Bible provides a universal judgment.
The Great White Throne is a demand of humanity
in a last appeal to the divine justice. That Christianity meets this instinctive demand is a presumption in its favor.

But when the infidel blots out eternity he blots
out relief and reconcilement. He sweeps away hope.
He admits that evil must triumph over good. He
believes injustice inevitable, and warps his own sense
of right  He involves the universe in everlasting
moral confusion, and leaves for himself only despair.
Nothing remains for him but mad rebellion, or cold
and hard and sullen submission to a pitiless inex-
orable necessity. For such a moral condition suicide is the legitimate remedy. That cannot be
truth which leads thus to life's wreck.

Speculating on the mystery of the pain problem
of creation, Voltaire and Hume and Huxley and
Darwin and Ingersoll resemble children puzzling
over questions only to be solved by manhood. They
apply a terrestrial capacity to difficulties celestial in-
tellects may never comprehend. An archangel may
not have a key to the whole administration of the
moral universe. Before attempting science the boy
must learn his letters. Otherwise he babbles nonsense. Let our infidel infants wait a few thousand

years, and they may attain wisdom if they seek it modestly! No more than a scorner can a Christian solve all dark questions of animal and of human suffering, but he believes that the "Judge of all the earth will do right." While clouds hide his ways righteousness supports his throne. It is night above and rock below. With this faith in God the Christian quiets himself, and abides the appearance of the Great White Throne. Thus, if he has not always explanation, he has always relief.

Even this, however, is only a partial view of the comfort experienced when we turn from nature to the Bible. *There* the woe of creation is softened by the love of redemption. Through earth's darkness from paradise to judgment shine rays from the cross. With the primal curse was the primal promise. Over the cloud was the bow. Amid fire and storm and earthquake a still small voice! Universal Mercy precedes universal judgment. Infidelity separates creation from redemption. To it the world is rock without flower, night without day, disease without medicine, skeleton without flesh, death without life, despair without hope, the woes of time to be followed by no songs of eternity,

## VII

### ARCHÆOLOGICAL PROOFS

MODERN enterprise has explored Assyria, Egypt, Arabia, and also Palestine and the contiguous regions, with unexampled sagacity and success. The keys to the cuneiform and hieroglyphic writings have opened to us a knowledge of the very nations most constantly and intimately associated with the Hebrews. From Moses to Christ the Bible is confronted with the archæology accumulated by the industry and learning of our nineteenth century. Manners, customs, laws, art, science, literature, religion, geography, topography, have been investigated, and the life of the great oriental nations has been illustrated by pen and picture. An inscription on a tablet, a cylinder, a wall, a tomb, a column, a papyrus, may at any moment challenge Scripture. From ancient lands the very dust of death seems flying into the faces of its writers. Yet so far antiquity has not made one cloud upon their statements. On the contrary, after the most searching, and often hostile, scrutiny they are confirmed by testimonies from every age and every region heretofore explored.

From many facts I will adduce a few to show how modern research proves the scrupulous accuracy of the biblical record.

Scripture makes Armenia the center whence radiated earth's populations, and from Armenia Celt

6

and Goth and Slav and Scandinavian migrated
to Europe, and thence, too, issued the inhabitants
of China, Japan, and Hindustan. The analysis and
comparison of languages show close, subtle, and
numerous relationships between the Greek, the Latin,
the Teutonic tongues, and the Sanskrit of ancient India. Scripture and science unite thus in
testifying that from the lofty table-lands of Asia
the world was peopled, and that there was spoken
the original language of our race.

Over earth, in all ages, are discovered traces of a
universal monotheism. Archæology enables us to
begin our proof in Egypt. On the scroll of a papyrus found in a tomb is the record of a creed more
ancient than pantheism or polytheism. "Nuk-pu-
nuk!" What mean these words expressing primitive belief on the Nile? *"I am that I am!"* Just what
Moses heard from the flame of the bush!

In the Assyrian Pantheon Asshur was worshiped
as the *one* supreme God.

India bears testimony to a faith older than the
dream of Buddha. Her Dravidians sang:

> " God the Omniscient fills all space
> And time ; he cannot die, nor end. In him
> All things exist. There is no God but he—
> *One, inseparate.*"

Before Confucianism, before Taoism, before all
other religious and philosophic systems, also in China
existed the same primitive monotheism.

Nor was the oldest and purest creed of Greece

different! The words of Sophocles sound down the
ages like utterances of a Hebrew prophet:

> "*One*, in very truth, God is *one*
> Who made the heavens and the far-stretching sea,
> The deep's blue billow and the might of winds."

And the Roman sibyl gave her voice to celebrate
the unity of the Deity:

> " Know and lay up wisdom in your hearts !
> There is *one* God who sends rains and winds and earthquakes,
> Thunderbolts, famines, plagues, and dismal sorrows,
> Over heaven he rules and earth, and truly is."

Hence it follows that the divine unity which is the
doctrine of Scripture was originally the doctrine of
humanity until corrupted by polytheism into idolatry, as we now see in the recovered creation—records of Assyria marred by names of many gods.

The early postdiluvians in Genesis said: "Let us
make brick and burn them thoroughly. They had
brick for stone and slime for mortar." Now, the
Egyptians built their temples, palaces, pyramids, and
monuments from their quarries on the hills east of
the Nile. And this fact gave character to their
whole architecture. But the Assyrians were too
far from the Armenian mountains to transport stone.
Just as first described by Moses they made "brick."
Nineveh and Babylon were *brick*. All the cities of
the Mesopotamian plain were *brick*. Always and
everywhere, as in the nice prophetic touch of the
biblical historian—*"brick for stone and slime for
mortar!"*

How often have the shafts of infidelity been hurled against the Pentateuch where it describes at Babel the confusion of tongues! Sneers, scorn, ridicule have been chosen arguments to demolish Scripture. Strangely, at its favorite point of assault against the citadel of inspiration modern skepticism is met by a wonderful modern discovery. The mound of Birs Nimrud furnishes proof that on the very remains of the tower of Babel itself was erected, by the most celebrated Chaldean builder and conqueror, his "temple of the seven lights of the earth." I will give you his inscription, which I ask you to compare with the Mosaic account of the confusion of speech:

"Nebuchadnezzar, king of Babylon, shepherd of the peoples, the repairer of the pyramid of the tower —the temple of heaven and earth—I have adorned in the form of a cupola of shining gold—*for the other a former king built it, but he did not complete its head. Since a remote time people have abandoned it without order expressing their words—I set my hand to finish and exalt its head.*"

Abraham led a wandering life like that of a Bedouin chief. He lived in tents, and owned flocks amid a primitive patriarchal simplicity. But he differed from the barbaric leader of wild hordes. He showed the culture, courtesy, and dignity which come from education. Only a superior and disciplined intellect could have left on all ages the impress of so majestic a character. But whence the cultivation of this nomadic chief? Recent explorations furnish the answer. Ur, the native city of

Abraham, was a splendid Chaldean metropolis. Stamped bricks reveal the names of many early kings. Urukh was a conqueror and builder second only to Nebuchadnezzar. He erected a temple from whose lofty towers astronomers observed the stars. Abraham was born and educated amid the highest culture of his times. But around him were the costly and imposing monuments of idolatry. False gods were the worship of his country. All the facts discovered harmonize with the call and character of Abraham as described in Scripture.

Permit me here to quote a remarkable testimony from Smith's *Assyrian Discoveries,* made interesting by the premature death of the gifted and enterprising author. He says:

"Among the new texts discovered during my expeditions to the valley of the Euphrates are several inscriptions of great importance belonging to the early kings of Babylonia. One of these is a new text of Assurbanipal relating to the restoration of the images of the goddess Nana. In the book of Genesis it is stated that in the time of Abraham Babylonia was under the dominion of Elam, and the monarch of the country bore the name of Chedorlaomer, or Kurdurlagamar. In the inscriptions of Assurbanipal, who reigned B. C. 668 to 626, we are told that when the Assyrian monarch took the city of Shushan, the capital of Elam, B. C. 645, he brought away from the city an image of the goddess Nana, which had been carried off from the city of Erech by Kurdur-Nahundi, the Elamite monarch at the time of the Elamite conquest of Babylonia, 1,635 years before, *thus confirming the statement of Genesis that there was an early conquest of Babylonia by the Elamites."*

In Kings and Chronicles we are informed that Rezin, king of Damascus, and Pekah, king of Israel, were allied against Ahaz, king of Judah, who invoked aid from Tiglath-pileser. An historical tablet discovered at Nimroud confirms minutely the biblical narratives. To perpetuate the glory of his conquests Tiglath-pileser says:

"Of Rezin, king of Syria, eighteen talents of gold, three hundred talents of silver, two hundred talents of copper I appointed. Damascus his city I besieged; like a caged bird I inclosed him, Pekah their king; and Hoshea to the kingdom over them I appointed—the tribute of them I received."

In the twentieth chapter of Isaiah we read: "In the year that Tartan came unto Ashdod (when Sargon the king of Assyria sent him), and fought against Ashdod, and took it." Sargon! who is he? What history records the name and reign of this Assyrian monarch *once* mentioned in Scripture? Greek, Latin, Hebrew writers! Examine them all! You can find no trace of Sargon. His name had perished from the historic page. Then Isaiah unconfirmed is Isaiah mistaken! For two thousand years there was no answer to infidelity. Skeptic and Christian were alike ignorant. Yet there was a record, but it was hidden from view by the soil of ages. M. Botta, in 1842, began those excavations at Khorsabad which preceded the more brilliant and illustrious discoveries of Layard. The first monuments brought to the light were those of this vanished Sargon. He was one of the most magnificent of the Assyrian conquerors. Although small, his palace was scarcely exceeded in ornamentation by any royal edifice. But Isaiah says that Sargon "fought against Ashdod and took it." And now an octagonal cylinder discovered by Mr. George Smith records this very conquest of Sargon mentioned by the Hebrew prophet. Believers and scorners of Scripture are taught here a lesson of patient waiting for evidence which is impressed by every advance of modern archæology. Let me now give you the inscription of Sargon which so accords with Isaiah:

"In my ninth expedition to the land beside the great sea to Philistia and *Ashdod* I went—the cities of *Ashdod* and Gimzo of the *Ashdodites* I besieged and captured."

Scripture tells us "that Sennacherib came up against all the fenced cities of Judah and took them," and in his inscription Sennacherib says of his expedition against Hezekiah, "Forty-six of his strong cities I captured." Biblical record and Assyrian cylinder agree precisely. But Sennacherib was not to take the Hebrew metropolis. Jehovah had declared to Isaiah, "Therefore thus saith the Lord concerning the king of Assyria, He shall not come into this city—by the way that he came the same shall he return." Now, the glory of a conqueror is the pos-

session of the capital of his enemy. Compared with
this achievement, provincial towns and spoils are
nothing. Had Sennacherib seized Jerusalem and
fettered her king, in the boastful style of an oriental
despot, he would have emblazoned his victory in his
inscriptions. He says that he made Hezekiah like
a caged bird in his royal city. He says that he
raised towers around the Hebrew metropolis. He
says that he shut the exit of the great gate. He says
that he detached Judah to the kings of Ashdod,
Gaza, and Ekron. He says that he conquered Hezekiah, and overwhelmed him with the fear of the
might of his dominion. Isaiah asserts that Sennacherib should not enter Jerusalem, and Sennacherib asserts everything but that he did enter Jerusalem.

Chronicles have a record which long seemed irreconcilable with historic facts: "Wherefore the Lord
brought upon them the captains of the host of the
king of Assyria, which took Manasseh among the
thorns and bound him with fetters, and carried him
to Babylon." But the metropolis of the conquering
monarch was Nineveh. And were not Nineveh and
Babylon rivals and enemies? How could the king
of Nineveh convey his captive to Babylon, the capital of his foes? The writer in Chronicles is surely
in error! So it appeared for centuries. No man
living had an explanation. Now the cloud is lifted
and the Bible proved to be correct. Inscriptions
show that Esarhaddon, king of Nineveh, held Babylon as his tributary and transferred to the subject

city the throne of his empire. Living in Babylon,
he conveyed to Babylon Manasseh, his royal prisoner.

The great work of Maspero gives us another proof
of Scripture accuracy. In the nineteenth verse of
the fifteenth chapter of Second Kings it is said:
"Pul, king of Assyria, came up against the land."
But Assyria never had a king named Pul. In Babylon only was a king styled Pul, and here it was a
favorite national title. This was long a puzzle for
biblical critics. Was the inspired word mistaken?
Until recently there was no answer. But a late discovery makes all plain. The dynastic lists show that
Tiglath-pileser conquered Chaldea. To soothe their
pride and compliment the victor the Babylonians
gave the king of Assyria the chosen and peculiar
title of their own monarchs. Thus in the Bible he
was properly called PUL. We may add that the
royal honor conferred on Tiglath-pileser III was
continued in Shalmaneser V, his son.

Belshazzar was the last king of the magnificent
Chaldean metropolis. Nothing in any literature
is more graphic than the description of his tragic
death by Daniel. The banquet, the finger writing
on the wall an empire's doom, the terror of the monarch, the interpretation of the prophet, the end of
the dynasty in the blood of its ruler make a picture
which will live in art and religion through all time.
But only in the Bible does the name of Belshazzar
occur. In vain you search for it in history. How
could it happen that a monarch terminating a dy-

nasty by so signal a catastrophe could thus sink into oblivion? Here again for more than two thousand years was a strong case against the reliability of the Bible. Daniel has blundered! So the skeptic decided, and it appeared a just verdict. Not until the year 1854 did the explanation come. In a temple of the moon Sir Henry Rawlinson found an inscription which informs us that Nabonadius, the usurper who succeeded Nebuchadnezzar, married his daughter and associated with himself on the throne of Babylon his son Belshazzar. Nabonadius before its fall left the city and conducted the defense against Cyrus without the walls, while Belshazzar remained within and was killed as described by Daniel. Although grandson, by oriental usage he was styled son of Nebuchadnezzar. Another thing has been made plain. Belshazzar promised Daniel to reward a correct interpretation by making him *third* ruler in his kingdom. The father Nabonadius was first, the son Belshazzar was second, and this left the third place for Daniel.

War and captivity brought the Jews into close and frequent association with the Assyrians. How powerful the impression through Nebuchadnezzar and Darius by Daniel on the Chaldean and Persian empires! Nineveh and Babylon are conspicuous in the vivid imagery of prophets and on the sober pages of historians. From the mountains of Armenia to the shores of the ocean the vast plain of Mesopotamia became connected with the Hebrew people. And now that memorable region has been made the scene of extensive explorations. Tombs and temples and palaces of the old cities in the valleys of the Tigris and Euphrates have been examined, and afford us varied and vivid pictures of dim and distant centuries. Under such circumstances mistakes in the biblical writers would inevitably have been discovered and exposed. We have already produced instances of minute and wonderful confirmation. And the whole effect of Assyrian research has been not only to strengthen faith in the Scripture, but to shed light on passages before obscure, and even unintelligible.

When we turn from Assyria to Egypt coincidences multiply. The land of the Nile more even than the valley of the Euphrates was associated with the history of the Hebrews. Abraham, father of his nation, sojourned in Egypt. Next to the throne Joseph had his seat and wielded royal power. Old Jacob found refuge under the shadow of Pharaoh. Four hundred years of captivity connected the Hebrews only too intimately with their masters. Moses was educated in a palace of the most splendid of the monarch-conquerors, who, from the valley of the Nile, extended empire over a large part of Asia and Africa. The national life of the Hebrew for centuries was blended with the national life of the Egyptian. And the peculiarities of the latter were most numerous and striking. Annual overflows of the Nile gave direction to life along the river. Embalmment of the dead imparted eccentricity to the habits of the people who kept mummies in their homes. The worship of beasts affected religious character. In dress, in manners, in arts, in literature, in philosophy, the Egyptians were distinguished from all other nations, and pictured on their tombs their daily lives are vividly visible. Inscriptions on wall and obelisk, and the writings of their papyri increase our familiarity with the country of the Pharaohs. Yet each fresh discovery along the Nile proves how faithful were the delineations of the sacred penman. A Jew by blood, in knowledge Moses was an Egyptian. Only birth and education in the land could insure an exactitude that never fails. The Egypt of the Bible is the Egypt disclosed by the archæologist.

To illustrate what has been advanced we will select a few facts from the Exodus. It will be perceived that the reigns of the great Rameses and Meneptha his son furnish all the conditions necessary for the occurrence of the events recorded in the scriptural narrative.

Moses describes the lives of the Israelites as a bitter bondage. They were oppressed by toil and cruelty. A cry of woe went up from their hearts to Jehovah. Now we find from the monuments that the suffering of the people depicted in Exodus is just what might be expected under Rameses. He proves to have been a haughty, remorseless, exacting tyrant. Diminished and exhausted by war, he yet forced his people to erect numerous and stupendous works. A papyrus of his reign shows the intolerable miseries of his kingly oppression. Hewn from rock at Ipsamboul colossal images of himself were monuments of his victories. The porch of majestic Karnak was covered with his battles. His sculptures filled the Theban Ramesseum, where gods in stone offered homage to this intolerable mortal despot. In the temple of Ptha rose enormous statues of himself and his queen, and Tanis bore witness to his lavish expenditures. Canals, sphinxes, obelisks over Egypt attest his tireless enterprise and boundless extravagance. Nearly every ruin along the Nile bears the name of Rameses, whose collective works rival the pyramids. But he bought his glory with the toil and tears and blood of his people. Especially by labor and punishment did he waste and torture his captives. On the graves of men he reared the temples of his gods.

More than all others did the Israelites suffer. Papyri and monuments show that the gigantic Asian wars of Rameses were in self-defense. His empire was threatened by a powerful confederacy. The land of Goshen, occupied by the Israelites, was the key to the military situation. His Hebrew slaves could open to the Asian foes of Rameses the gates of his empire. Goshen, too, furnished his army supplies. Here were vast quantities of grain stored in magazines. The tyrant feared that the Israelites would seek freedom by inviting his enemies from Asia into Egypt, and hence he wished to reduce his slaves by exacting toil and cruel oppression. Thus modern research reveals all the social and political conditions which give reality and animation to the book of Exodus.

We have seen that the wars and works of Rameses exhausted his kingdom. But during his life his bold military genius restrained the popular tempest. His death loosed storm and earthquake, and his son Meneptha paid the price of his father's glory. More than ever feared the Hebrew slaves of Goshen between Asia and Egypt who commanded the entrance to the kingdom of the Pharaohs, and who by joining their foes could shake the throne and secure liberty! Meneptha became a gloomy and suspicious tyrant. He sought by increased toil, enforced by stripes, to break the spirit of his bondmen, and to reduce their numbers by the murder of their children. In the struggle between the monarch and Moses, in the plagues, in the flight, the pursuit, the escape, the destruction, and in each topographical detail by land and sea, modern research casts over the picture that lurid light befitting the overthrow of a tyrant predestined to his ruin.

The harmonies do not cease when we pass into the wilderness. From Nile to Sinai and from Sinai to Jordan the journey has been followed and explained. The historian of the Exodus was familiar with that terrible and desolate region. How exquisite his local coloring! How faithful his masterful pencil! When we read the old biblical narrative we are amid scenes so vividly depicted by the modern traveler.

I will select a single but most striking proof.

The place of the declaration of the Law was a mountain. Around it were encamped two millions of people. In the region of Sinai is there a spot which can accommodate this multitude and meet the other conditions of the narrative? The country is a scene of wild, gigantic, volcanic mountains. Innumerable peaks lift brows of ragged rocks into heaven. In immense regions not a valley would accommodate the Hebrew host. Piled and seamed with splintered rocks, the narrow gorges are bounded by walls of perpendicular granite. Travelers long sought in vain to discover a place such as the Mosaic narrative required. Volumes were written, and theories were endless. Finally, to settle the question, an expedition was sent out under the British Ordnance Survey. Thus was secured a trained military experience. Two captains of Royal Engineers were of the party, and also one of the most learned professors of Arabic in the world. By months of labor the entire region about Sinai was surveyed and mapped. A peak was discovered which unanimously the party decided as uniting all the requirements of the record of Moses. Its picture makes visible the correctness of their opinion. From the midst of a valley amply wide and level for the Hebrew encampment, abrupt as the sides of an altar, we see Ras-Susafah, the rival of Jebel Musa, lifting itself in solitary grandeur, fitted in every way to be that summit on which the elect nation witnessed the cloud and storm and fire, when amid thunders the Law was given to Moses by Jehovah.

Entering Palestine, we find that every hill and vale and stream and ruin has been examined. Jew

and Greek, Protestant and Romanist, men of every
sect and of every nation have been visiting the Holy
Land during centuries. Travelers and residents,
pilgrims and warriors, believers and infidels have
united in the search. The Land and the Book have
been indefatigably compared. Recently has been
applied a crucial test. An English Palestine Ex-
ploring Fund is devoted to the critical examination
of Judea, and a committee a few years since was appointed to search the sacred soil with an unsparing
scrutiny. The substructions of the temple of Jerusalem have been laboriously examined. Beneath ac-
cumulations of centuries walls, vaults, sewers,
arches, galleries were discovered and described.
Royal Engineers here too brought the enterprise and
exactitude and experience of the military profession.
Their measurements and drawings evince the greatest accuracy attainable in this age of science and
art. Every discovery harmonizes with the Bible.
Indeed, the reports of the explorers are now necessary to a complete understanding of the scriptural
records. Amid a vast mass of confirmatory knowledge one slight fact is of inestimable importance.
Its insignificance gives point and power to its testimony.

In the account of the erection of the temple the
builders supplied by Hiram, king of Tyre, are said to
have *"hewed"* part of the stones used in the structure. And these "hewed stones" were not prepared
at the place, but *"brought* to the foundations." Now,
stones hewed at a distance must have quarry marks

to indicate their position in the building. Also stones hewed by Phœnician workmen would have Phœnician quarry marks. How wonderfully the recent explorations prove these conditions to have been met! Amid the earliest substructions of the temple are foundation stones with Phœnician letters in red paint, fresh after the concealment of centuries, and plainly Phœnician quarry marks made by the Phœnician builders.

## Tel el Amarna Tablets.

Infidelity once affirmed that there was no culture in the era of Moses which could produce the Pentateuch. A recent discovery dispels the objection. Cuneiform tablets unearthed at Tel el Amarna, in Egypt, contain the correspondence of a Pharaoh with an Assyrian monarch. We have also letters proving that Palestine was ruled from the banks of the Nile. Epistles between the Egyptian king and his Judean agents are in the cuneiform character. When Joshua conquered Canaan it had an advanced civilization and literature, with the Aramaic script, which, perhaps, prevailed over the Orient. On the upper Euphrates was Carchemish, capital of the powerful Hittite empire, and possessing a hieroglyphic language resembling that of Egypt. We have all the literary conditions, also, to confirm the Jewish tradition that Moses composed Job, which, like the pyramids, is peerless in sublimity. The book required the loftiest poetic genius. Moses, we know from his songs, had the divine gift. The book

7

is in Hebrew, and a Hebrew was Moses. The book pictures behemoth and leviathan, monsters of the Nile. Moses lived on the Nile. The book describes vividly the wild ass with desert and mountain for his range, and the war horse, whose terrible nostrils, and neck clothed with thunder, and excitement at the noise of the trumpet and the clash of battle almost transport us into Arabia; and Moses was familiar with Arabia.

We will complete these isolated proofs by coming down far into the history of the world. The inter-mediate testimonies are beyond our power to enu-merate.

In the book of Acts we have a most vivid picture of a popular tumult in Ephesus. It raged in defense of the temple of Artemis, by the Latins styled Di-ana. A shrine maker, whose craft was endangered by Paul's assaults against idolatry, excited his fel-low-artisans to guard the honor of the goddess, the object of their peculiar worship and the author of the wealth, fame, and magnificence of their city. The people rush to the theater ready to murder Paul. Wild and furious cries succeed. We perceive in the tumult all the excesses of a democracy.

After more than twelve years of labor and peril an English architect, Mr. Wood, has uncovered the ruins of the temple of Artemis. In his search for the site of the buried edifice he found on the marbles of a theater inscriptions which reveal the life of Eph-esus for five centuries. Strangely it is shown that the city had a democratic constitution bestowed by

its tyrant-conqueror, Alexander the Great. The recovered records harmonize with this original constitution. All begins and ends with the people.
The citizen dominates the assembly. And each inscription for centuries accords with the picture of
Paul in the Acts. The very local words translated
"town clerk" and "temple keeper" are found on the
Ephesian marbles and in the scriptural narrative.

# VIII

## AUTHENTICITY OF THE OLD TESTAMENT

On the shelf of my library I see an English Bible. It contains the books of the *canon* of the Old and New Testaments. What do I mean by *canon?* It is from the Greek κανών, signifying *rule*, and occurs once in Corinthians, once in Galatians, and once in Philippians. Earliest among the ancient fathers St. Clement and St. Irenæus employed the word to denote the whole number of the sacred books, and from them it passed into universal currency.

In regard to the books of the Bible I often hear the words authentic, genuine, and credible. What is *authentic?* What is *genuine?* What is *credible?* I answer, a book is *authentic* when written by the author whose name it bears; *genuine,* when not a forgery and the name of the author is lost; *credible,* when true without respect to its author. A book, therefore, may be authentic and credible, genuine and credible, and neither authentic nor genuine and yet credible; or it may be authentic or genuine and nevertheless not credible.

Whatever the work, sacred or profane, questions concerning its authenticity must be determined by virtually the same methods. I greatly admire the fiery eloquence of the oration against Catiline by Cicero. How can I determine whether it was delivered by the illustrious Roman in the senate chamber of the Capitol? I trace it from age to age. I find it lauded, quoted, expounded, transcribed, published back to the time of the orator himself. I read his allusions in his letters to his friend Atticus. Moreover, it bears every mark of the country, period, and genius of Cicero. I am as certain that Cicero is the author of the oration against Catiline as I am of any fact in the universe.

In regard to all other books investigations may be more or less extensive, complicated, and conclusive, yet they must be by methods similar to those I have just described. I will return to the Bible on my shelf. An inquiry suggests itself. I wish to know whether it can be proved that the books of the Old Testament contained in my English version were in those Hebrew Scriptures expounded and authorized by Jesus Christ. Let this be noted! My sole object is to trace the Old Testament of my Bible to the time and knowledge of that Man of Nazareth who claims by his resurrection to have proved himself the world's Redeemer. I do not at present touch the question of credibility. It is only genuineness and authenticity that I now proceed to examine.

From my shelf I take down the book I would investigate. I turn to its title-page. There I read these words: "The Holy Bible, containing the Old and New Testaments, translated out of the original tongues, and with the former translations diligently compared and revised." Former translations! What are these? This inquiry takes me back into the century beyond the time of James the First, who was the patron of my English Bible. I find its predecessors. Chiefly these were the Bishop's Bible, the Geneva Bible, Tyndale's Bible, Coverdale's Bible, and, if I pass into Germany, Luther's Bible. The common source of all these translations was the Hebrew Scriptures as used in every Jewish synagogue in the world. Now, in my inquiry, Jew and Christian have the same interest and may follow the same methods. Side by side with any learned rabbi I may prosecute my investigations.

Pushing onward into the centuries of the past beyond the Reformation, I ascertain that there were then known nearly seven hundred manuscripts of the Hebrew Scriptures in various states of completeness, and preserved in Spain, in Italy, in Germany, in Russia, in England, in the Orient. And passing yet further, we reach the

### Masora.

After the destruction of Jerusalem, and the dispersion of the Jews over the Roman empire, schools were established for the study of the Hebrew Scriptures. An academy at Tiberias became specially distinguished. Here the rabbis collected the learning of centuries to determine the true reading of the Old Testament text. Their work was called the Masora, or Tradition. Its notes and criticisms relate to vowels, points, and accents. They even counted how often each letter occurs in the Hebrew Scriptures, proved by these learned labors to have existed as early, perhaps, as the seventh century.

Long before, toward the close of the second century, Rabbi Judah completed the digest of the oral law and tradition called the

## TALMUD.

As the Masora was intended to fix the true text of the Hebrew Scriptures, so the Talmud was intended to fix the true interpretation. Quoting from them accurately and extensively, it becomes an incontestable witness to their existence. The Talmud consists of the Mishna, or text, and the Gemara, or commentary. Its traditions are ascribed by the Jews to early periods of their history. Some claim that Moses received them on the mountain of the Law. But without reference to its origin or authority the Talmud enables us to trace the Old Testament to the second century before Christ.

Before describing the Targums we will mention the

## HEXAPLA OF ORIGEN.

Only fragments of this work exist. These are invaluable for our argument. Beyond cavil they establish the fact for which we seek proof. Origen was the most learned, original, and brilliant of the Greek Fathers. In any age he would have been a marvel of genius and erudition. He devoted twenty-eight years of his laborious life to collecting and collating manuscripts. Out of this long and learned toil grew the Hexapla, which will be for all time a monument of proof in behalf of the Scriptures. This great work, begun in A. D. 231, was finished in A. D. 260, its name being derived from εξ and

*ἁπλόος*, meaning *six* and *fold*. The Hexapla contained, 1. The Hebrew text; 2. A text in which
Greek letters were substituted for Hebrew; 3. The
version of Aquila; 4. The version of Symmachus;
5. The Septuagint; 6. The version of Theodotion.
Here we may introduce

### JOSEPHUS.

He was a contemporary of apostles. In his trea-
tise against Apion this great Jewish writer mentions several books of the Old Testament. His
*Jewish Antiquities* are largely compiled from the
sacred writings.

### PHILO,

in the first century of our era, cites or names nearly all the books of the Old Testament. Beyond
him, about fifty years before Jesus Christ, we reach
the

### TARGUMS.

These are paraphrases of the various parts of the
Old Testament in the East Aramaic dialect. When
in the synagogue the Law was read in Hebrew it
was rendered into this Aramaic, which after the captivity had gradually become the language of the
Jewish people. Out of this custom grew the ten
Targums. Of these two only need be mentioned:

1. The Targum of Onkelos. He is supposed to
have been a disciple of the celebrated Rabbi Hillel,
and to have lived about a half century before Christ.
The work of Onkelos renders each Hebrew word accurately, and is confined to the Pentateuch.

2. The Targum of Jonathan Ben Uzziel, also a disciple of Hillel. It treats of Joshua, Judges, Samuel, and Kings, called the "Former Prophets," and of Isaiah, Jeremiah, and Ezekiel, with the twelve minor prophets, this whole second part being designated the "Latter Prophets."

Together the Targums of Onkelos and Uzziel paraphrase nearly the whole of the Old Testament, and prove its existence among the Jews fifty years before the birth of Jesus Christ.

According to the universal tradition of the Jews, Ezra collected all the books of the sacred writers as they now stand in the Hebrew Scriptures. Accept this view, and five hundred years before Christ the canon of the Old Testament was complete. After the Babylonish captivity synagogues were erected in every part of Judea, and in these their Scriptures were read and expounded to the people. Indeed, as the Jews spread over the world they made this custom universal. And they thus claim that from the age of Ezra to this hour, on each Sabbath of the year, the Hebrew Scriptures have been used to explain the Hebrew faith in Hebrew synagogues. It is not necessary to our argument that we pause to defend the Jewish belief. Without this, we have shown all we now wish to prove—that the Hebrew Bible was that to which appeal was made by Jesus Christ.

We have now exhausted our *first* line of investigation, and enter upon a second, which is different and independent. Along another path we reach the same result, and trace the Hebrew Bible to the era and knowledge of Jesus Christ.

On the shelf of my library I see another volume. I take it from its place, and discover it to be in Latin. The title-page informs me that it is the

## VULGATE.

My curiosity is excited. I begin my *second* line of inquiry. What is the Vulgate? It is the sole standard of the Roman Catholic Church. In the sixteenth century the Council of Trent gave formal and final authority to the usage of ages. Hear the words of its famous canon in regard to the Vulgate:

"It shall be deemed authentic in the public readings of the Scriptures, in disputations, in preaching and expounding, and no one shall dare reject it under any pretext whatever."

Before the decree of Trent Pope Sixtus V had issued an edition of the Vulgate anathematizing all who would not acknowledge it as without error. Wyclif in the latter part of the fourteenth century translated it into English. It circulated in Europe through all the Middle Ages, and received the approbation of Pope Gregory the Great in the sixth century. The Vulgate was made in the fourth century under the patronage of Pope Damasus. Nothing can be better known than its history. Its author was the celebrated St. Jerome, born at Stridon, in Dalmatia. An early passion for rhetoric and philosophy led him to the courts and schools. The literature of pagan Rome exerted over him a fascination,

In his dreams he was reproached for wishing to be
a Ciceronian rather than a Christian. After long
and terrible struggles he devoted his life to the Holy
Scriptures. At Chalcis, a hermit in his solitary cell,
he learned Greek and Hebrew. Invited to Rome,
he was induced by Pope Damasus to give himself
to the revision of the Old Italic version of the Bible.
Afterward he made the tour of Palestine, and in a
monastery of Bethlehem began his grand work. We
have seen that the Vulgate of Jerome was based
on the

## Old Italic.

At the beginning of the Christian era the Latin
commenced to supplant the Greek as an interna-
tional language. Many translations of the Scripture were made from the Greek into Latin. Parts
of separate versions became united. Marginal notes
crept into the text. Diversity produced confusion.
Gradually other translations were superseded by the
superior fidelity and excellence of the Old Italic,
which obtained universal circulation in the Latin
Church until displaced by the yet greater merit of
the Vulgate. The Old Testament was probably
from the Septuagint and translated in the early part
of the second century, to which date also belongs
another version which must have been known to
Jerome, and which is styled the

## Peshito.

This is Syriac, and has also a most venerable
authority. But both Italic and Peshito imply a He-

brew original, and thus by this second path of investigation we trace the Hebrew Scriptures to the era of Jesus Christ.

We are now prepared for a *third* distinct line of inquiry. I lift my eyes again to the shelf of my library and remark a volume larger than my Vulgate. The title is in Latin. Translated into English, I read, "The Old Testament according to the Seventy Interpreters." Here confronts me the

## SEPTUAGINT.

On examination I find that the text is Greek. As the Vulgate is the standard of the Occidental, so the Septuagint is the standard of the Oriental Church. I go back in the history of the world three centuries. I pass the period of the Reformation. I traverse the Middle Ages. I travel to the time of Justinian and hear the Septuagint before Mohammed changed St. Sophia into a mosque and the cross into the crescent. I know that it was read in the Basilica of Constantine; that it was in the Hexapla of Origen; that it was used by the Jews in every part of the old Roman imperial world, and quoted by fathers, apostles, and even by Jesus Christ. Before his time for centuries it had been in the Jewish home, the Jewish school, the Jewish synagogue in every region of our earth where Greek was the spoken language and the Jewish people found a mart for trade or a refuge from persecution.

It is therefore important to know the history of the Septuagint. The sword of Alexander carved for it a way over the world. His conquests in Asia and Africa by the enlargement of the Greek empire extended the use of the Greek language. Alexandria became the new capital of Egypt. The patronage of the Ptolemies converted their metropolis into a brilliant center of commerce and learning. Jews swarmed to Alexandria. Since their Babylonish captivity they had been gradually losing command of their native Hebrew, which then, as now, was mastered only by their rabbis. Hence arose a necessity for translating their Scriptures into Greek. This was accomplished by the munificence of Ptolemy himself. The Septuagint was thus made, according to Josephus, nearly three centuries before Christ, in the isle of Pharos, near Alexandria, either by seventy-two Jews brought by the royal command from Palestine for the benefit of the royal library, or by seventy-two members of the Alexandrian Sanhedrin for the use of the Alexandrian Jews, or for the mingled purpose of promoting Greek learning and Hebrew convenience. But even accepting the modern hypercritic view, long before our era the thirty-nine canonical books of our authorized English version were translated from Hebrew into Greek. Since, the Septuagint has maintained itself in every part of our globe. It is a universal book. It proves that the Old Testament existed in the time of Jesus Christ, and three hundred years before his birth.

The Jews considered the sacred oracles their peculiar trust from Jehovah. Guardianship of Scripture was their boast and glory. Never has the purity of any writings been protected with such a zealous care. The books of Moses were deposited in the ark for preservation, and also by command taught the households of Israel. A special copy was made for the king. So exact and reverential were the Jews that a distinct order of men was consecrated to the work of transcribing the national oracles. Among the scribes those who copied Scripture performed no other labor. The name of Jehovah was ineffable. Mortal pen might not write it. The Jewish copyist substituted for it Adonai. So fearful was the scribe of disturbing the text that obvious errors were indicated in the margin. After the captivity the Scriptures were statedly read in the synagogues. We have thus an invincible argument for the authenticity of the Hebrew oracles. Nor can we doubt that the Jews were best qualified to settle their own canon. It is safe to receive the books which they received, and to reject the books which they rejected. And Christ as a Jew accepted the Hebrew Scriptures approved and circulated by his countrymen.

We have seen how the purity of the text of the Old Testament was guarded. Forgery was less easy than corruption. The Pentateuch records the beginning of the Jewish nation in the Abrahamic covenant. It narrates the origin of circumcision, a rite enjoined by Moses on Joshua and since observed throughout the Hebrew world. Moreover, the Pentateuch describes the plagues of Egypt, the passage of the Red Sea, the announcement of the Law, the erection of the tabernacle, the appointment of the priesthood, and the apportionment of Canaan among the twelve tribes of Israel. Joshua narrates the crossing of Jordan and the conquest and settlement of the promised land. Both Moses and Joshua appeal to the nation as witnesses of the recorded facts. The other books of the Old Testament continue the Jewish history until the return from Babylon and the rebuilding of Jerusalem. As to Job, the Ecclesiastes, the Canticles, and also the prophets with their burning denunciations of idolatries and every other national sin, and their terrible predictions of punishment, there could be few inducements to forgery.

We will suppose, for illustration, that a thousand years after the events it describes an impostor had sought to impose a fabricated Pentateuch on the Hebrew people. Could such a forgery deceive the Jews? We can answer by considering a similar attempt on ourselves. Could we be persuaded to receive into our national records narrations of our colonial and revolutionary times forged and false? Could we credit accounts of battles never fought, settlements never made, treaties never signed, defeats never experienced, victories never won, compromises and adjustments and confederacies which never existed, and of a Constitution never created, and of laws never enacted? Could we be induced to believe that our fathers were actors in imaginary events, and had left us records and memorials of which we had never heard? Impossible! And if we could not be deceived by such forged histories, the Jews could not be deceived by such forged histories. They are the oldest people in existence, the most famous, and the most widely scattered. They are united in an organization with rites and ceremonies practiced for ages. For the origin and history of their national institutions they refer to the Old Testament. Shall we not receive their testimony transmitted from their ancestors and believed in all generations? If we reject it, we are presented with an unexampled spectacle. That nation, most renowned for its antiquity, for its religion, for its literature, for its customs and its influence, is without a history.

From the same library we have had three starting points. These were the English Version, the Vulgate Version, and the Septuagint Version. Beginning at each, we have passed along the centuries, and have traced the Old Testament to the hand of Jesus Christ. To this evidence might have been added proofs from quotations, from catalogues, from commentaries, from readings, from manuscripts, from heretic and from infidel, and from many incidental sources. It was unnecessary to our argument. We only wished to show that the Old Testament was known to our Saviour.

## IX

### AUTHENTICITY OF THE EVANGELICAL HISTORIES

THE Gospels and the Acts we include under the title Evangelical Histories. Proofs of their authenticity apply to the whole of the New Testament, but some explanations would be required in regard to several epistles and to the Apocalypse, which were received later into the canon. To avoid interruption in our argument we will therefore confine ourselves to the Evangelical Histories. But these are of transcendent importance. Especially are the gospels the center of all proof and of all doctrine. They claim to fulfill the Messianic prophecies of the Old Testament, and they furnish those Messianic facts which are the life of the New Testament. On the Evangelical Histories, then, must be based the supreme and sufficient argument for Christianity.

Here, then, we reach the question of prime importance: What are the proofs of the authenticity of the Evangelical Histories?

I will begin with the

### MANUSCRIPTS.

Of these there are hundreds in different languages. They are usually not earlier than the tenth century. It will only be necessary to describe a few which are the most ancient and celebrated:

8

## Codex Ephremi.

This is a manuscript in vellum or calfskin in the library of Paris. Probably it is of the sixth century. The first part contains several Greek works of Ephraim the Syrian, and hence the name of the codex. It is a rescriptus, or palimpsest, having been written over a Septuagint so imperfectly erased that letters intermingled with the old text produce confusion. The Codex Ephremi is an Alexandrian recension of the New Testament in Greek of great purity. Although it has many gaps, it proves that in the sixth century existed all the Evangelical Histories. Most likely it is of Egyptian origin.

## Codex Cantabrigiensis

is perhaps a hundred years earlier than the Codex Ephremi. This manuscript is in the Greek and in Latin, and contains the Gospels and the Acts. It is in the library of the University of Cambridge, to which it was presented in 1581 by Theodore Beza, having been found in the Monastery of St. Irenæus, in Lyons. This traces to the fifth century the Evangelical Histories.

## Codex Alexandrinus

is in four folio volumes. The first three contain the Old Testament with the apocryphal books, and the fourth has the New Testament together with the Epistle of St. Clement. All are in Greek. The Alexandrinus was probably written in the fifth century. Its great antiquity is universally conceded.

This venerable codex was brought from Alexandria in 1628 by Cyrillus Lucaris, Patriarch of Constantinople, and presented to Charles the First through Sir Thomas Rowe, the English ambassador. In 1753 it was deposited in the British Museum, where it is now preserved. It shows that perhaps as early as the fifth century the Evangelical Histories were in circulation.

### Codex Vaticanus.

This contained originally the entire Bible in Greek. Usually it is assigned to the fifth century, but, influenced by many agreements with the Codex Sinaiticus, scholars incline to believe that the Vaticanus was made by the imperial command of the Great Constantine as recorded by his friend and eulogist, the historian Eusebius, Bishop of Cæsarea. This invaluable manuscript is in the Vatican Library, at Rome. From the Old and New Testaments are now wanting in it forty-six chapters of Genesis, thirty-two Psalms, and parts of the epistles to Timothy, Titus, Philemon, and Hebrews, and the Apocalypse. Accepting the most recent opinions of scholarship, it shows us in the fourth century the Evangelical Histories.

### Codex Sinaiticus.

It is in Greek, and contains the Old Testament and the New Testament, the latter being perfect. Tischendorf discovered the manuscript in 1869 in the Convent of St. Catherine, on Mt. Sinai, and it is in the imperial library of St. Petersburg. The authority of the Sinaiticus equals the authority of the Vaticanus, and both are now believed to have originated in the order of the Emperor Constantine for fifty copies of the Scripture to be made under the superintendence of Eusebius.

By means of the great manuscripts we have traced to the beginning of the fourth century all the Evangelical Histories. Then follow the

## CATALOGUES.

Rufinus, Presbyter of Acquileia, in the latter part of the fourth century, left a catalogue of the books of the Old and New Testaments, adding, "These are the volumes which the Fathers included in the canon, and out of which they would have us prove the doctrine of the faith."

About the same time, in Africa, St. Augustine, most celebrated of the Latin Fathers, published a list enumerating the books now found in our own English Bible, and including no others.

St. Jerome, author of the Vulgate, also about the middle of the fourth century, supplied a catalogue similar to those of Augustine and Rufinus, only with the intimation of a doubt in regard to the Apocalypse.

Philostratus, Bishop of Brescia, in the year 380, gives a catalogue also identical with our own, except that it omits Hebrews and the Apocalypse, by some doubted, but by him esteemed canonical.

Gregory Nazianzen, Bishop of Constantinople, in the same year, enumerates the books of the New Testament except the Apocalypse, which, however, he quoted in some of his other works.

The Council of Laodicea, about the year 350, issued a catalogue agreeing with our own except in the omission of the Apocalypse.

Eusebius, Bishop of Cæsarea, in the beginning of the fourth century, published a catalogue embracing our present books, mentioning, however, that the Epistle of St. James, the Second of St. Peter, the Third of St. John, and the Apocalypse, while questioned by some, were yet generally received, and in his opinion properly.

Cyril, Bishop of Jerusalem, made a catalogue like our own except in the omission of the Apocalypse.

Athanasius, Bishop of Alexandria, and the illustrious adversary of Arius, furnished a catalogue of the books of the New Testament which are precisely those we now esteem canonical.

Origen, the most learned of all the Fathers, in the earlier part of the third century, made the first complete transmitted catalogue. It agrees with our present canon.

The Muratorian Fragment is nearly a century before Origen, and is the earliest of all the catalogues. It was discovered in the Ambrosian Library of Milan in a manuscript of the seventh or eighth century, but came from the Monastery of Columbari, at Boblio. Muratori, whose name it bears, published it about 1740 in his *Antiquitates Italicæ*. Although not mentioned, the Gospel of St. Matthew evidently stood first in the canon. The Fragment commences with a reference to the Gospel of St. Mark. St. Luke is third in order, and fourth follows St. John. The book of Acts is mentioned as containing a record by St. Luke "of those acts of all the apostles which fell under his notice."

We have thus in these catalogues, extending to about the middle of the second century, proof of the existence of the Evangelical Histories.

## COMMENTARIES.

Of these were various kinds on the different books of the New Testament. In the fourth century there were fourteen expositions. Julius Africanus, Ammonius, and Origen wrote epistles, harmonies, and commentaries on the sacred books. Eusebius, in the year 300, says: "There remain divers monuments of the laudable industry of those *ancient* ecclesiastical men, besides treatises of many others whose names we have not been able to learn, orthodox and ecclesiastical men, as the interpretation of the divine Scriptures given by each of them shows."

As early as the year 170 Tatian began the list of expository writers. He was followed by Pantænus, a man of distinguished learning, and the illustrious Clement of Alexandria.

## HERETICS.

The Gnostics made their appearance during the life of the apostle John. Numerous wild and fanatical sects disturbed the early ages of the Church. These assaulted the orthodox faith, and were answered in writings which compose a learned and extensive literature. All parties appealed to the Scriptures as a standard, and thus furnish incidental but incontestable evidence of the authenticity of the Evangelical Histories.

## INFIDELS.

Julian the apostate noticed by name St. Matthew, St. Luke, and St. John, and also events in the Acts about three centuries after the publication of the Evangelical Histories.

Porphyry, a century before Julian, made an attack on Christianity. He urges objections against passages in St. Matthew, St. Mark, and St. John, and also in the Acts composed by St. Luke, thus establishing as previous to his own times the existence of all the writers of the Evangelical Histories.

Celsus, a hundred years earlier, in an effort to overthrow the authority of the Evangelical Histories, has perpetuated indubitable testimony to their authenticity. He says, "I could say many things concerning the affairs of Jesus, and different from those written by the disciples of Jesus." He accuses Christians of altering their Gospels, takes notice of their genealogies, and assails their precepts.

## PUBLIC READINGS.

Augustine says, "The canonical books of Scripture being read everywhere, the miracles therein recorded are well known to the people."

Cyprian tells us, "Nothing can be more fit than

that he who has made a glorious confession of the Lord should read publicly in the church—that he who has shown himself ready to die a martyr should read the Gospel of Christ by which martyrs are made."

Origen bears witness, "Thus we do when the Scriptures are read in the Church, and when the discourse for explanation is delivered to the people."

Tertullian, before Origen, testified, "We come together to recollect the divine Scriptures; we nourish our faith, we rouse our hope, confirm our trust by the sacred word."

Justin Martyr, one hundred and forty years after our Saviour, wrote, "The memoirs of the apostles" —called by him in other places Gospels—"or the writings of the prophets are read according as time allows. When the reader has ended the president makes discourse exhorting to excellent things."

Irenæus, Bishop of Lyons, before the close of the second century epitomized Christianity in a

## CREED.

His is the earliest authenticated attempt to summarize the facts and doctrines of the Evangelical Histories, and presumes their existence and diffusion. We will give the creed of Irenæus, because it expresses the consciousness of the Church, which could only have been shaped by long and familiar acquaintance with the Gospels:

"The Church, though dispersed throughout all the world, hath received from the apostles and their disciples the faith in one God, the Father Almighty, and in one Christ Jesus, the Son of God, who became incarnate for our salvation, and in the Holy Spirit, who proclaimed through prophets the dispensation of God, and the advents, and the birth from a virgin, and the passion, and the resurrection from the dead, and the ascension into heaven in the flesh of the beloved Jesus our Lord, and his future manifestation from heaven in the glory of the Father, to gather all things into one and to raise up anew all flesh of the whole human race, in order that to Christ Jesus our Lord and God and Saviour and King, according to the will of the invisible Father, every knee should bow of things in heaven and things in earth and things under the earth, and that every tongue should confess him, and that he should execute just judgment toward all."

The Creed of Melito, a contemporary of Irenæus, shows also how his age had become saturated with the truths of the Evangelical Histories:

"We have made collections from the Law and the Prophets relative to those things which have been declared respecting our Lord Jesus Christ, that we may prove to your love that he is perfect Reason—the Word of God, who was begotten before the light; who was the fashioner of man; who was all in all; who among patriarchs was Patriarch; who in the Law was the Law; among priests, Chief Priest; among kings, Governor; among prophets, the Prophet; among angels, the Archangel; in voice, the Word; among spirits, Spirit; in the Father, the Son;

in God, God: the King forever and ever. For this
was he who was Pilot to Noah; who conducted
Abraham; who was bound with Isaac; who was
exile with Jacob; who was sold with Joseph; who
was captain with Moses; who was director of the in-
heritance with Joshua, the son of Nun; who in David
and the Prophets foretold his own sufferings; who
was incarnate in the Virgin; who was born at Bethlehem; who was wrapped in swaddling clothes in
a manger; who was seen of shepherds; who was
glorified of angels; who was worshiped by magi;
who was pointed out by John; who assembled the
apostles; who preached the kingdom; who healed
the maimed; who gave sight to the blind; who raised
the dead; who appeared in the temple; who was believed on by the people; who was betrayed by Judas;
who was laid hold on by the priests; who was condemned by Pilate; who was pierced in the flesh;
who was hanged on the tree; who was buried in the
earth; who rose from the dead; who appeared unto
the apostles; who ascended into heaven; who sit-
teth on the right hand of the Father; who is the rest
of those that are departed—God who is God; the
Son who is of the Father; Jesus Christ, the King
forever and ever. Amen!"

## Versions.

The Vulgate of the fourth century, the Old Italic
and Peshito of the earlier part of the second, all
bear testimony to the Evangelical Histories.

## Quotations.

St. Clement, about eighty years after the death of our Saviour, in his two epistles, quotes St. Matthew nine times, St. Luke four times, and the Acts once.

St. Ignatius, a few years later, in his acknowledged epistles, quotes St. Matthew nineteen times, St. Luke seven times, St. John twenty-nine times, and the Acts five times.

St. Barnabas quotes St. Matthew twice, St. Mark once, and St. John once.

St. Polycarp, in his epistle to the Philippians, quotes St. Matthew seven times, St. Luke once, and the Acts once.

But the force of the argument can only be realized by extracts from these venerable authors called Apostolic Fathers because they lived in apostolic times.

From St. Matthew plainly St. Clement quotes: "Be merciful, that ye may obtain mercy; forgive, that it may be forgiven you; as ye do, it shall be done unto you; as ye judge, so shall ye be judged; as ye are kind, so kindness shall be shown unto you; with what measure ye mete, with the same it shall be measured to you."

St. Ignatius could supply many quotations from the Evangelical Histories. The books from which the following extracts are taken will be obvious to all readers of the New Testament:

"For the tree is known by its fruit. As Jonah was three days and three nights in the whale's belly, so shall the Son of man be three days and three nights in the heart of the earth. For there are many wolves in sheep's clothing. Be ye perfect, as your Father in heaven is perfect. For a spirit hath not flesh and bones, as ye see me have. Thou shalt love the Lord thy God, and thy neighbor as thyself. I am the way and the life. I have glorified thee upon the earth; I have finished the work thou gavest me. The Word was made flesh. I can of my own self do nothing. Father, forgive them! they know not what they do. Watch ye, and be sober. The disciples were called Christians at Antioch. It is hard to kick against the pricks." Paul is called "a chosen vessel." "This same Jesus who is taken from you into heaven shall so come in like manner as ye have seen him go into heaven."

St. Barnabas precedes a quotation from St. Matthew by saying, "It is written, Many are called, but few are chosen." He has also words contained in the first three Gospels: "He came not to call the righteous, but sinners to repentance."

St. Polycarp affords the following: "Who raised up from the dead, having loosed the bonds of the grave. The spirit truly is willing, but the flesh is weak. Judge not, that ye be not judged. Blessed are the poor and those that are persecuted for righteousness' sake, for theirs is the kingdom of God."

After the Apostolic Fathers quotations of the ecclesiastical writers become so numerous that we could restore the substance of the Scripture should every copy in the world be obliterated.

## EUSEBIUS AND PAPIAS.

The former, as we have seen, was the learned Bishop of Cæsarea and an intimate friend of the great Constantine. His *Ecclesiastical History* is one of the most interesting monuments of his times. It was written before 325, the year of the Nicene Council.

Eusebius has preserved a most remarkable extract from Papias:

"For I have never, like many, delighted to hear those that tell many things, but those that teach the truth. Neither those that record foreign precepts, but those that are given by the Lord to our faith and that came from the truth itself. But if I met with anyone who had been a follower of the elders anywhere, I made it a point to inquire what were the declarations of the elders—what was said by Andrew, Peter, or Philip; what by Thomas, James, John, Matthew, or any other disciple of the Lord."

Observe! Papias saw and heard men who saw and heard the apostles of Jesus Christ. He had conversed, therefore, with those acquainted with the authors of the Evangelical Histories. Knowing those who knew the original writers, possessing such unusual opportunities for securing certitude, a witness such as rarely exists for any ancient authorship, what says Papias? Hear his clear and conclusive testimony!

"Matthew composed his history in the Hebrew dialect, and everyone translated it as he was able. Mark being the interpreter of Peter, whatsoever he

recorded he wrote with great accuracy, but not, however, in the order in which it was spoken and done
by the Lord, but, as before said, he was in company
with Peter, who gave him instruction as was necessary."

But, it is objected, this testimony applies to but
Matthew and Mark; nothing is said of John and
Luke. Besides, Eusebius lived three centuries after
Papias, who was himself a witness of not great
mental force. This brings us to a proof which
crowns our argument.

## IRENÆUS AND POLYCARP.

Here we have together the Bishop of Lyons and
the Bishop of Smyrna—the first a man not only of
vast learning, but of great intellectual power, directed by a sound judgment; and the second a martyr
proved sincere and sensible by all the circumstances
of his touching and tragical death. We could have
no more reliable and venerable witnesses to the authenticity of any book. They bring the authorship
of the Gospels directly to the writers whose names
they bear in our English Bibles.

Of his opportunities for knowledge Irenæus testifies:

"But Polycarp also was not only instructed by
apostles, and conversed with many who had seen
Christ, but was also in Asia by apostles appointed
bishop of the church of Smyrna, whom I also saw
in my early youth, for he tarried a very long time,
and when a very old man suffering martyrdom de-

parted this life, having always taught the things he had heard from the apostles, and which the Church has handed down, and which alone are true."

Polycarp, who heard the apostles, instructed Irenæus. But Irenæus ascribes the Evangelical Histories to apostles whom Polycarp knew. I give you the words of Irenæus which fix the authorship of the Gospels:

"John relates his original, effectual, and glorious generation from the Father, thus declaring: In the beginning was the Word, and the Word was with God, and the Word was God. Luke, taking up his priestly character, commenced with Zacharias the priest offering sacrifice to God. Matthew again relates his generation as a man, saying, 'The book of the generation of Jesus, the son of David, the son of Abraham.' Mark, on the other hand, commences with the prophetical spirit from on high, saying, 'The beginning of the Gospel of Jesus Christ, as it is written in Esaias the prophet.'"

But in addition to this unanswerable cumulative evidence it is certain that the Gospels and the Acts could only have been written within a brief period after the death of Jesus Christ. The conquests of Alexander had diffused the Greek language, and the conquests of Pompey had diffused the Latin language among the Jews, whose spoken language after the captivity was the Aramaic, a corruption of Hebrew with Chaldee. To make his proclamation intelligible to all the people Pilate placed above the cross words in Hebrew, Greek, and Latin, which depict the social and political condition of the Jewish nation. The inscription over Christ sprang from that condition, and in that condition only was possible. But we find a similar condition in every part of the Evangelical Histories. These are filled with allusions which presume the Aramaic, or corrupted Hebrew, as the speech of the Jews, the Greek as a familiar language, and the Latin as the tongue of conquerors. I will specify! How often occur in the Evangelical Histories *centurion,* and *prætor*, and *proconsul,* and *Cæsar,* and *Augustus,* and *other similar terms!* Proofs these of a Latin domination! We may illustrate in the same way from the Greek and the Hebrew. The Evangelical Histories are in Greek, yet not in classic Greek, but in just such a Judaized Greek as would have been written in those times and by those authors, and could have been written in no other times and by no other authors. Everywhere are visible in the Gospels and Acts traces of the three nationalities which prevailed in the country. Land and Book and Era harmonize. A century after the ruin of city and temple the style of the Evangelical Histories would have been impossible.

One other consideration concludes our argument. The Church extends over the world. Her existence is the most potent fact in human history. After centuries of strife that filled earth with flame and blood and death the Church has deepened and widened her sway over man. And she promises to dominate our race. She has her oracles, her sacraments, her ministers, her observances. Could such an institution be without a history? Shall she not know her own origin? Shall she possess no record of her rise and struggle and spread? To the Evangelical Histories she refers us for the narrative of her birth, her growth, and her authority. She has no other and knows no other, and there is no other. Her writers and councils, representing the world's best ability and erudition, from the beginning of Christianity have ascribed to their present reputed authors the Evangelical Histories. The Church is thus a perpetual witness to the authenticity of the five fundamental books on which she rests her faith, and no other writings have ever had in their behalf such an array of cumulative and invincible evidence.

9

## X
## ADAPTATION OF CHRISTIANITY

A RELIGION from heaven should meet the universal needs of our humanity. Such a requisite is fundamental and indispensable. Is God my Omniscient Creator? Then he knows my nature, and will make provision for it corresponding to his infinite power and wisdom. A religion from God will bear the impress of God. It will immeasurably transcend all human systems, and be known by its perfect adaptation to all human wants. Reason can judge this claim to our attention. Before presenting the positive proofs of Christianity, permit me to show that it is a religion having the visible signature of God because so wisely and completely suited to man.

I will begin with a lesson from idolatry itself. In the human heart is a powerful tendency to worship through images. Pictures and statues please the eye and excite the fancy, and by their grace and beauty attract multitudes to temples where they are supposed to assist in the contemplation of the invisible Supreme. Owing to their abuse in sensualizing and degrading the soul, they are forbidden by the Mosaic Law, and yet after ages of command and instruction idolatry still has in our world a large majority of votaries. It must therefore testify to some universal need in man. What does each carved and pictured image in the pagan temple witness? A desire in our race for faith in some being superior to our humanity, and deserving its trust and worship. Yet by her canvas and her marble idolatry cannot satisfy this yearning of man. The mind grows out of its superstition, and scorns the image it adored. Gods even in the beautiful and majestic forms of Greece could not appease the cry of the soul. Always at last it overthrows the divinities it creates.

Now, Christianity acknowledges the need to which idolatry testifies. To meet that need is the first and fundamental provision of Christianity. And surely there is strong presumption in behalf of that religion, which, admitting the universal need witnessed by idolatry, makes to that need its prime appeal by presenting as an object of faith and love and adoration a Being at once Creator and Sovereign of the universe: in his existence, eternal; in his presence, power, and knowledge, without a limit; in his justice, in his mercy, in every conceivable perfection, immeasurable and unsurpassable. Imagination itself cannot transcend the excellence of such a provision. Christianity lifts man to the dream and ideal of his soul. His heart wants the Infinite for trust. His reason wants the Infinite as a cause for nature. His imagination wants the Infinite to satisfy his aspiration for perfection. In his fear and impotency, amid change and death, awed by the vastness of the universe and the shadow of eternity, man reaches out to the Infinite for help with a cry which will not be stifled, and Christianity, like a mother, cares for this frail and unfortunate human infant. She points not to the carved or the painted image, nor to saint, nor to angel, but to the Infinite God as the object of trust and worship.

But by the idol of the temple stands the *altar*. In its blood and flame what is expressed? Life is given to expiate sin. How powerful the impulse which overcomes the selfish greed in man, and destroys his property by knife and fire? Rivers of blood flow in atonement. Flames of sacrifice make lurid our world. This blind demand for propitiation is indeed pitiable superstition. But it is in human nature a deep, overmastering force not to be overlooked. It expresses the very soul of man, and has always been at the root of his most popular and powerful religions. Christianity recognizes this mighty need of our race. Consider the expiation she offers! Wide as the realm of light or gravitation is the sway of the moral law. To meet its claim Christianity points to Jesus on his cross as a satisfaction to the eternal justice of Godhead, and also as a proof of the eternal love of Godhead, by the offer of a human life exalted to infinite worth by an everlasting union with Godhead. Only folly can mock such a scheme. It appeals to the most profound need of our humanity, and commands our attention, and secures our respect, and inspires with a desire to investigate its awful and sublime claims to our acceptance.

In addition to image and altar idolatry has her *laver*. What meant the sacred water of the temple? Here we meet a significance deep as that of blood. Water is man's universal symbol of purity. The laver shows the wish to escape moral defilement. Among the ancients lustrations by water cleansed individuals, cities, kingdoms, empires. Now, the Brahman's life is to avoid pollution, and the Ganges is the laver of India. The ablution of the Moslem precedes his prayers. In all ages and races, by varied rites, humanity expresses its painful and pervading consciousness of moral impurity, and its yearning and struggle for moral deliverance. Water, however, is the sign and not the substance. The laver in the Jewish temple was a prophetic symbol of what Christianity was to supply, not for a nation, but a race. A religion for humanity must offer something deeper than bodily baptism. Here Christianity has another claim to our regard. She would penetrate the soul and renew it by the power of its Creator. Not only does she offer pardon for guilt, but strives to restore our lapsed and defiled humanity by the energy of a divine regeneration. In her provision for our moral renovation by the Holy Spirit she increases her title to our respectful consideration.

Often, also, in the temple of idolatry was to be found the *oracle*. Man yearns to know the will of heaven. Is the god propitious? Is my gift accepted? Is my life approved? From my past and my present what will be my future? Humanity asks these questions. The oracle reveals the soul. But idolatry cannot lift the cloud of doubt from man. She can give no assurance of acceptance. Her oracle has proved a fraud or a failure. Over the pagan world is a dark shadow of conscious guilt. In the Old Testament by sacrifice in tabernacle and temple Jehovah promised pardon, and in the New Testament through faith in the atonement of Christ we are assured of forgiveness and regeneration, and the witness of the Holy Spirit that the everlasting God is our reconciled Father. We are no longer orphans in the universe, but sons and daughters of the Almighty. This grand provision for the soul of man is another powerful presumption in favor of Christianity.

Idolatry has another characteristic not yet noticed. She, too, passed beyond images to incarnations. An infinite spiritual essence is too lofty a conception for human apprehension. The sublimity of God must be reduced to the feebleness of man. But how contemptible the infleshed Jupiters of idolatry! They are mere mortal men with a varnish of divinity. Yet they testify the wish to make the deity appreciable by human deeds and words. And in answer to this profound and universal desire of man is the Incarnation of Christianity. It professes to accomplish that in which all other religions have failed. It submits to the world the birth and life and death and resurrection of Christ with proofs that in the lowliness of his humanity was the majesty of Godhead. It presents Jesus as the perceptible Jehovah. Adapted to so deep and wide a need in man, Christianity attracts to the investigation of evidences to establish her authority as a revelation from heaven.

Over image, altar, laver, and oracle in her temple idolatry throws the veil of mystery. She would

not have her gods and rites too familiar. Man is
awed as well as pleased. By every aid of art mystery
is impressed on the soul. Christianity does not overlook this tendency in humanity. Her provision for
it is the crown of her system. Above us forever will
be the sublime mystery of the TRINITY.

Idolatry testifies to a MORAL LAW. In her broken
mirror is a shattered image of eternal truth. But
each reflection is obscured by the mists of passion
or the pride of reason. Conscience in the human
breast was never silenced. Yet in the lives and
writings of the most virtuous pagan philosophers
what gropings in moral gloom! What bewilder-
ments of error! What inextricable confusions of
right and wrong amid sentiments most pure and
sublime! In their loftiest estate they showed human nature a splendid moral ruin. Oppressed by
darkness, they waited and yearned and prayed for
light. No spectacle in the universe sad as Socrates
longing for a spiritual illumination he never received. Whatever their merits, ancient philosophies
wanted *authority*. Only a sovereign can impose
law. Now, the Scriptures profess to appease the
cry of humanity for moral illumination by a light
of truth from God. The Old Testament announces
law amid fire and cloud and lightning and thunder
and tempest and earthquake from Jehovah, and the
New Testament announces law in the precept and
example of Jesus. The Bible presents itself as a
moral statute book from the Almighty Creator with
his sanctions of life and death everlasting. On per-

sonal beings it enjoins personal responsibility to a personal Sovereign. Love to God and neighbor sums all. This is the law of child and archangel. Our duty to an earthly parent illustrates our allegiance to the Father of the universe. And this simple and sublime moral system made practical, impressive, and beautiful in the life and death of Jesus Christ! What could more commend his religion to our consideration?

Idolatry had her emblems of *immortality*. A winged circle in Assyria symbolized eternity. The Egyptian papyri give us pilgrimages of the soul through the infernal hemisphere, and formularies for the worship of the dead. Greece had her Olympian and Plutonian regions, and from her Rome borrowed images of the realms across the grave. Gods and ghosts of Homer and Virgil indicate existence after this life. In his odes Pindar assumes that the dead live, and the grand lesson of Greek tragedy was retribution hereafter. The ancients conceived the departed soul as a magnet, a fire, a light, as air, as water, as number, as harmony, as a star, as the essence of motion. But when Plato and Socrates and Cicero would prove immortality by argument we see how dark the abysses of doubt into which they plunged for blind and hopeless struggle. Confronted with the mysteries of life and death, the belief of the purest and wisest of the ancients was exchanged for the lethargy of a dumb despair.

On childish platitudes Socrates based his faith in a future life. However we respect his creed, we

smile at his arguments. He proves immortality
by a play of words, or deduces it from the fable of
the soul's transmigrations. With such supports for
faith we do not wonder that Socrates, amid the tor-
pors of death, sacrificed a cock to Esculapius, and
expressed that doubt as to a hereafter which over
the ancient world cast a gloom from the midnight
of the soul.

Did Cicero seem to glow with confidence in immortality? It was the enthusiasm of the orator.
How flimsy his hope in a hereafter! A vision of
his imagination. He had no strength from argument. In his villa, amid his books, surrounded by
friends and luxuries, fresh from his triumphs in the
senate chamber, fancy kindled his pen, and his eloquence seemed inspired, but under the shadow
of misfortune his unmanly tears and gloom made
him a spectacle of laughter and contempt for his own
times and all ages. After his sonorous and splendid
sentences, radiant with immortality, he consoled
himself and his friends with the prospect of abso-
lute insensibility in death.

The question of immortality is insoluble by philosophy. Shall man risk his eternity on the fact
that spring revives flowers and changes worms into
butterflies? Perverted into arguments, such illustrations become contemptible. Nor does desire for
immortality establish the fact of immortality. Innumerable desires have no satisfaction, so that the
presence of a desire is no proof of its satisfaction.
To our human reason the subject is involved in

mist and mystery. To mortals over the grave is an impenetrable shadow. The stiff limb, the dumb lip, the blank face, give impression of an extinguished soul.

Like no other system, Christianity proposes immortality. She unfolds it as the end of a remedial scheme from eternity designed by the Sovereign Creator, disclosed dimly in the beginnings of our race, brightening ages by type and promise and prediction, and converging itself into a divine Saviour whose resurrection, proved by witnesses, is a pledge and symbol of a glory in his own everlasting image, and an ideal exceeding every mortal thought, aspiration, and imagination. This sublime and comprehensive plan is not an expedient to meet an emergency, but the predetermined purpose of the Almighty to which our world, and perhaps our universe, is subordinate.

With such a divine origin, ordination, and end, the scheme of Christianity is described as the center of all human history, the key to all human progress, the answer to all human speculations, the secret of all human felicity, and the clew and guide and test of each human life. It excites also our esteem by the wise reserve, the exquisite delicacy, the fidelity of justice, and the tenderness of mercy, the aptness and grandeur and majesty with which, in matchless words and images, it depicts a judgment for our world, and the consequent everlasting state of men where the equities of the divine administration will be visibly vindicated before the universe.

Nor does Christianity present itself as a speculation. It is not the system of a philosopher. It is not a dogma of schools. But it claims to be a revelation of the will of the Almighty, and impressed with his authority as Sovereign Creator. It therefore requires authentication. Like philosophical opinions, it could not rest on philosophical arguments. So supported it would sink into a human system. He who would represent the will of God must show credentials from God. Only thus can he secure faith in his mission. The scriptural appeal to Omniscience in the prophecy and to Omnipotence in the miracle was unavoidable. The ambassador from Jehovah must exhibit the signature of Jehovah.

Christianity differs from all other religions. They are without proof. Idolatry attempts no argument. Subjected to scrutinies of reason, all false systems dissolve into superstitions. But Christianity rests on facts. She does not transport us to Porch, or Lyceum, or Academy for philosophical discussion, but surrounds us with the witnesses of a risen and ascended Saviour, and on the plain principles of legal evidence challenges reason to investigate her testimony. Her proofs are from eye and ear and finger. All the rays of her types, promises, prophecies, and miracles she converges on the Person of Jesus Christ. She concentrates her past, her present, and her future on a Person. She embodies her doctrine in a Person. She expresses her spirit in a Person. She causes all the magnificence of her supernatural evidence to revolve, like a firmament of stars, about a Person. Her propitiation is by the death of a Person. Her moral system is exemplified in a Person. Her immortality lives in a Person. Her glory in heaven is from a risen and ascended and enthroned Person. All her joys, employments, and exultations during everlasting ages, as rays from the sun, have their source and center in a Person who is the visible symbol of Godhead for his universe.

The volume in which Christianity is conserved and diffused deserves our consideration. In its human aspect the Bible is venerable as the accumulation of the wisdom of centuries. Sublimely it records the creation of our world. But from paradise to judgment its grand object is salvation. Penned by writers from every class of society and with every variety of genius, and representing ages of the world's history, it is adapted to every grade of intelligence. While often rising naturally into a matchless beauty and sublimity of expression, and to the heights of loftiest argument, its words at once illuminate the reason, console the heart, touch the sensibilities, impress the memory, and exalt the imagination. It is a book loved by the poor, studied by the learned, praised even by the skeptic, read by all nations, suited to all races and ages, a guide in morals, a help in trouble, a companion in solitude, a chart and a compass for time's voyage toward the everlasting. The Bible is thus a fitting depository of the truths of salvation, suited to man and worthy of God. Its character is a potent presumption disposing to examine its title to a divine inspiration and authority.

Nor has Christianity been cast carelessly on the billows of time. Its Scriptures have been committed to the ark of the Church. Like human compositions, its oracles were not left to the prejudices of changeful generations. Always the Bible has been guarded by an organization. Under the old dispensation it was watched by the Jewish priest, and under the new dispensation is proclaimed by the Christian minister. Over the world it is brought to head and heart and life by all the power of human intelligence and human sympathy. Christianity is no waif on the solitary waters. It points to a conserving and witnessing Church, and thus predisposes to a scheme perpetuated and disseminated by such admirable and venerable wisdom.

Christianity seems to embrace whatever is desirable or possible in a religion. A revelation of the existence, government, and perfections of an Almighty Creator! In the death of a Divine Saviour infinite satisfaction to the eternal justice of Godhead and infinite manifestation of the eternal love of Godhead! A race redeemed! Pardon for all who accept! Renewal of man by the power of God! A divine witness of forgiveness! A divine law! A divine light! A divine example! A divine volume! A divine Church! Immortality through a divine Saviour! Orphaned man joyful in the fatherhood of God!

Existence of desire does not prove, but indicates a satisfying object. Vegetables and animals are supplied with what is needful for their organisms. Man for his physical and intellectual wants finds provision. His eye needs light and has light. His ear needs air and has air. His blood needs oxygen and has oxygen. His body needs food and has food. His heart needs love and has love. His mind needs knowledge and has knowledge. Does not analogy carry him onward to his spiritual yearnings? Shall his cry for pardon, purity, trust, worship, immortality be stifled? Then he was made to be mocked and tortured by his holiest, deepest, loftiest, mightiest desires. Then he was made with a soul which is a purposed and necessary void. Then he was made to be a waif in the universe. Shall man turn to paganism? He cannot go backward to that midnight of exploded superstition. Paganism is a dumb witness to wants it can never supply. Centuries have proved the impotence of philosophy to resolve our questionings about God and Immortality. Shall we seek refuge in the materialisms of science? In mathematics and machineries man cannot find what he may love and adore forever. Agnosticism is despair. It can no more repress the cry of a soul than it can drive back with straws the waves of the ocean, stop with dust the fires of a volcano, arrest with breath the revolutions of our world. For man it is Christianity, or hunger everlasting.

In establishing a law of the universe science demands that the proof be irresistible. Speculations of Copernicus in regard to the sun as the center of our system were insufficient. Evidence to the eye by Galileo's telescope concluded the inquiry. The laws of Kepler were not accepted until demonstrated by the mathematics of Newton. Proofs of Science must be clear, cogent, overwhelming. But the truths she establishes may be forever beyond her grasp. She can tell you the laws of force, the laws of light, the laws of electricity, the laws of soul, but can no more tell you what force is, what light is, what electricity is, what soul is, than she can tell you what God is. Each path to the temple of Science must be straight and plain, but within her edifice we are dwarfed by our ignorance, and awed by the magnitude and the majesty of the universe.

It is the same with Christianity. Always she follows the analogies of Science. The proofs of the Bible we will show you to be clear, simple, and convincing, while the truths of the Bible are often incomprehensible as the Godhead revealed. Deity only understands Deity. Before him inferior natures must bow in everlasting reverence. His glories unveiled would dazzle into blindness feeble worshipers in the temple of his creation.

# XI

## SUPERNATURAL EVIDENCE

.WE mean by supernatural evidence an interposition of the Deity to attest his Revelation. But Science urges that this is impossible. She establishes the reign of law. To her, phenomena of the universe are bound together in unbroken succession. Nor can she avoid recognizing this invariable sequence. Even discussions about cause and effect she leaves to philosophy, while theology lies wholly beyond her sphere. Induction from facts is the sole work of Science. Out of her province, an intruder, she soon turns tyrant, and sometimes persecutor. Yet she has a right to watch with suspicion the introduction of the supernatural into that rigid order which it is hers to study and confirm. Within just limits the jealousy of Science is commendable. Unless convincingly attested no man should credit a display of Omnipotence in the miracle and of Omniscience in the prophecy.

By what seem weak concessions advocates of Scripture sometimes seek to soften oppositions of Science. Apologetically, it is said the supernatural is not necessarily a violation of the order of nature, but may observe and overrule the order of nature for its purposes of evidence. They who urge such suggestions take an illustration from gravitation. This force draws to the earth a stone. I interpose my hand and arrest its fall. By my act I do not violate the law of gravity. I only counteract its attractive force by my physical force. Man, the mouse, the wren, the fly, even the animalculæ of a raindrop, are continually overcoming the gravitating power of the globe of the earth. And in the same way, to mind and muscle, we owe our triumphs over nature, marvelous to a barbarian as are miracles to a philosopher. Hence, it is argued, as man sets aside a lower law by a higher law, without violating law, so may the Deity act in supernatural attestations of his revelation. It is true that the Almighty Power *may* thus always work. But we are not assured as to his methods. He may reserve to himself illimitable liberty. As the explanation has no force as argument, so it does not touch the true point of inquiry. The question is not *how* the supernatural is exerted, but *is* the supernatural exerted? In our proof we deal with *fact* and not with *mode*. It is immaterial whether the laws of nature have been controlled, suspended, or violated. The sole inquiry is whether a miracle has been proved by the testimony of credible witnesses.

All divergences in regard to the supernatural arise from differing views of the Deity. By denying God atheism stops inquiry. Deism reaches the same result when it asserts God made the universe and, having wound up his vast machine, left it to be moved by its original impulse. Confounding God with the universe, pantheism affirms in nature one necessitated, undeviating, and everlasting succession. In each the fundamental principle makes supernatural evidence impossible. On the subject of miracle and

10

prophecy, with atheist, deist, and pantheist we can have no argument. With them premise contains conclusion, and definition denies divine interference.

But let me believe in a personal Creator! Let me believe that the universe was made by God! Let me believe that he is in all its parts to supply its force, ordain its laws, and accomplish its results! The Bible, then, to reason presents no difficulty. He who made the sun can stop the sun. He who made the sea can divide the sea. He who made man can heal man. He who made death can conquer death. He who made the world can burn the world and renew the world. Believing in God the supernatural is credible, and not believing in God the supernatural is impossible.

I will pass from general observations to specific objections urged against the miracles and prophecies of Scripture.

The celebrated argument of Mr. Hume has a touch of genius. It exhibits the resource and refinement of a philosophic mind. Like a seed, it includes all that has ever been urged against supernatural evidence by more gross and less original opposers of the Bible.

Permit me to give the words of Mr. Hume:

"Our belief in any fact from the testimony of an eyewitness is derived from no other principle than our experience in the veracity of human testimony. If the fact attested be miraculous, there arises a contest of two opposite experiences, or proof against proof. Now, a miracle is a violation of the laws of nature, and as a firm and unalterable experience has established these laws, the proof against a miracle, from the nature of the fact, is complete as any argument from experience can possibly be imagined, and if so, it is an undeniable consequence that it cannot be surmounted by any proof whatever derived from human testimony."

Mr. Hume constructs a logical balance. In one scale he places the fact that man falsifies, and in the other scale the fact that nature never falsifies. The testimony of nature, therefore, outweighs the testimony of man. Hence it is impossible by the testimony of man against the testimony of nature to establish a miracle.

No argument against Scripture was ever so ingenious, subtle, and plausible. But observe its foundation! Mr. Hume asserts that experience proves nature's order invariable. Whose experience? Does our argument-weigher mean his own experience, the experience of his readers and his generation? Granted! Does he mean the experience of centuries before his own age? Granted! Does he mean experience one hundred years after Christ? Granted! Does he mean the experience of the apostles who testify the resurrection of their Master? *This* is the fact at issue. Taking *this* for granted, Mr. Hume begs the question. We agree in regard to every period after Christ. The question does not include subsequent centuries. We inquire *only* whether witnesses in the *time of Jesus* saw his miracles; saw him after his resurrection; saw him ascend into heaven.

Mr. Hume, too, confounds experience with inexperience. Suppose in a trial for murder a *thousand* witnesses swear they did not see the accused stab the deceased! But they were not at the spot. Their inexperience is nothing. *One* witness testifies he saw the fatal stab. His experience proves the crime against the inexperience of the whole world. In supernatural evidence only few of mankind can have experience. Manifested to all, the supernatural would have no more force than the natural. Only infrequency gives value to miracles. The skeptic must make experience and inexperience identical before he can prove the impossibility of establishing miracles by human testimony.

And Mr. Hume's argument leads to absurdities. A few centuries since no man believed that the earth revolved about the sun. The eye was against the fact. Copernicus was opposed to the experience of the world. But the arguments of the reason overcame the testimony of the sight. Had Mr. Hume's speculation been accepted, the true system of astronomy could never have gained one adherent. Every savage could have urged his inexperience as a reason for his disbelief, and placed himself on a level with our prince of philosophic skeptics. His argument there is self-destructive. It sweeps away not only revealed religion, but inductive science, and would keep the world in the infancy of perpetual barbarism.

Strauss suggested a theory which has none of the ingenuity of Hume. He held that several centuries

after Christ, from the traditional myths of the
Church, the Evangelical Histories shaped themselves
into conformity to the career of the supposed Messiah of Old Testament prophecies. Such a theory
must be tested by facts. To me the arguments seem
overwhelming which show that before the close of
the first century the Evangelical Histories were composed by their reputed authors. If on the proofs
already submitted I cannot believe this, I can believe
nothing. There are skeptics with whom, on their
own principles, it is vain to reason. Denying the
supernatural, they seek by the natural to explain
Scripture. To me this task is impossible as to atheistic critics' belief in Revelation. With such men
the question is not the truth of the Bible, but the
existence of God. Having lost faith in him, facts
of creation are puzzling as the miracles and mysteries of redemption, and the end is the gloom of a
defeating and despairing doubt.

Dr. Carpenter, of the University of London, has
expanded an argument foreshadowed in his *Mental
Physiology*. He presents striking cases of sense-
illusion. Persons of shrewd intelligence, on the testimony of eye and ear, have credited as facts
things proved to have never occurred. In one instance a multitude was misled into the belief of a
spectacle of agony which existed only in imagination. They trusted their sight and were deceived.
Our senses are liable to daily impositions. Now, it
is urged that, in the same way, the miracles of the
Bible were illusions. The witnesses practiced de-

ceits upon themselves. But if the argument have force, it shakes confidence in whatever the senses testify. Are not the physical sciences founded on the very evidence the theory would discredit? Without the observations of the senses chemistry and geology and astronomy could have no existence. Disbelieve what your eye sees through the telescope, and a science of the heavens is impossible. Distrust your ear and your finger, and the telegraph is an unmeaning toy. The argument of Dr. Carpenter would close his laboratory, prove chemistry a deception, and build on illusion the splendid superstructure of our modern science.

Despite theories the senses are practically reliable. They are trusted every moment by the men who would shake faith in their testimony. We learn to discriminate. It is discovered that illusions and delusions are abnormal and infrequent. One sense corrects another, and over all reason stands sentinel. Belief in touch and taste and smell and sight and hearing becomes invincible and ineradicable in our humanity. It lies at the foundation of each individual life. It is at the basis of society. It supports the edifice of science, and may therefore without impropriety sustain the temple of religion.

Applied to the miracles of the Bible, the theory of sense-illusion is perceived to be absurd. Let us consider the flight from Egypt and the journey through the wilderness! Moses appeals to the Israelites as witnesses. Two millions of people saw the Nile turned into blood when it was always water; saw the air filled with locusts and the earth covered with vermin when neither had been infested; saw fire fall, and cattle killed, and the land darkened, and infants slain, whereas the whole was deception. Two millions of people persuaded themselves that for miles they had traveled between walls of water on the bottom of a sea guided by a cloud, and had sung in triumph at their emergence, when not a man had gone through the deep and not a note of exultation had been uttered. Two millions of people believed they received their law from a burning mountain, and ate food supplied during forty years in the wilderness, whereas not a word had been heard from the flame and thunder of Sinai, and not a crumb of manna fell to earth from heaven. Forged narratives are conceivable. But that multitudes, during nearly half a century, cheated themselves by sense-illusions which delivered them from peril and sustained them in existence is far more difficult to believe than narratives which record the facts as miracles wrought by an Omnipotent Creator.

M. Renan, a poet in prose, paints a picture better than he points an argument. He claims that in the supreme miracle of the resurrection of Jesus the heart seduced into deception the eye and the ear and the finger. After his death the affections of his disciples converted their buried Master into a living man. But the fanciful and brilliant Frenchman must state his own case:

"Death is so absurd a thing when it smites a man of genius, or the man of large heart, that people will not believe in the possibility of such an error on the part of nature. The little Christian society of that day worked a veritable miracle; they resuscitated Jesus in their hearts by the intense love which they bore toward him. The love of the passionate, fond souls is truly stronger than death, and as the characteristic of a passionate love is to be communicated, to light up like a torch a sentiment which resembles it, and is straightway indefinitely propagated, so Jesus, in one sense, at the time of which we are speaking, is already resuscitated."

Death an absurdity! Death nature's error! Death a disbelief! Just the reverse with our humanity! Death, like life, is *the* fact of our world. It is wrought into man's constitution. It is so universal and ineradicable that no sentiment can veil it for a moment in oblivion. It spares neither genius nor generosity, and admits no easy and patronizing allusions by a visionary.

Let us apply to ourselves the fancies of M. Renan! Our friend, a man of genius, expires. We follow him to his grave and witness his burial. Now, our passionate love persuades us that he lives. We walk with him, talk with him, embrace him under the spell of our affections, believing he is with us, while he is yet in his grave. A lunatic asylum would soon prove what the law thought of our heart-illusions. To summon phantoms from tombs; to impose on our memories words never spoken; to follow such imaginations for years, and sacrifice life for deceptions as facts, is impossible for sanity. And no man has ever yet called the apostles lunatics.

But what say the histories to which M. Renan is indebted for his narratives of the resurrection? Nothing is so marvelous as the incredulity ascribed to themselves by the witnesses except their own honesty in recording it. Instead of being deceived by their love they represent themselves as stolid in their unbelief. The pictures of the evangelists are the opposites of those painted by our modern literary artist. They describe the disciples as insensible to the most powerful proofs of the resurrection. Predictions which the enemies of Jesus remembered the friends of Jesus forgot. They bore in their hands to the sepulcher evidences of their want of faith. To embalm a corpse they brought spices. They expected to find a dead friend, not a living Lord. When the risen Jesus stood in their midst they shrank from him as a ghost. He had to assure them by appealing to his flesh and eating in their presence. For all time Thomas is a typical skeptic. Even on the mountain of Galilee, where the apostles received their grand commission, "some doubted."

Passing from particular objectors, we will now notice the connection of the supernatural system of the Scriptures with the moral system. The two are inseparable. Turn to the first verse of the Bible! It ascribes to God the creation of an elemental universe. Cycles followed crowded with the works of the Almighty Architect. A world is deluged and a race saved by a divine interposition. Covenants with patriarchs are made by the voice of Jehovah,

who scourges Egypt, divides the sea, moves in cloud
and fire, dwells visibly in tabernacle and temple.
Centuries are filled with prophecies of a Messiah
from birth to ascension claiming to be the manifested God. Do the Scriptures open with the supernatural? They close with the resurrection of our
race and the renewal of our world. Always the
moral is imbedded in the supernatural. Does the
Decalogue enjoin duty? It is delivered amid awful
displays of the divine majesty. Nearly every precept of our Saviour is related to a miracle. Does
he preach on a mountain? Before, he heals the sick,
and after he cures a leper. He shows his right over
the Sabbath by restoring a withered hand and making straight a deformed body. Does he sum all duty
in love to God and man? Preceding in the narrative is an illustration of the resurrection of the dead.
Would he show his human sympathy? He drops
a brother's tear before the grave from which he
commands a brother's life. How taught he charity? By feeding with miraculous bread a hungry
multitude. On his cross he shakes the earth and
darkens the sun, and gives his last token of love
while ascending into heaven.

Can you remove from the rock the shells that compose it? Can you take away its fibers and preserve
the tree? Can you separate without death the
minute cells from the body that build up its life?
Impossible! No more in the Bible can you wrench
the supernatural from the moral. Yet amid its miracles and its prophecies you find a matchless holi-

ness. Then the moral system is a presumption in favor of the supernatural system. Immaculate virtue would never link itself to detestable imposture.

Each miracle of the Bible teaches truth or impresses holiness. Puerile and contemptible the apocryphal and mediæval prodigies! Too often they bear the marks of avaricious or ambitious imposture. But the scriptural miracles are evolutions of a venerable system, extending through centuries, each performing its part in authenticating revelation, each having its place, each, like a stone in an edifice, giving strength to the majestic temple of truth. After filling the pockets of villains, and exciting the stare of the multitude, works of superstition pass away. Never do they become incorporated with the moral and intellectual development of humanity. Miracles of the Bible live. Designed chiefly to attest Christianity, they continue to enforce its moral system and guide its spiritual experiences. They teach at the fireside and glow in the pulpit. They become emblems of faith and love and hope, musical in song and beautiful in art. They are immortal as inspirations to genius and symbols of salvation.

Physical science and Scripture are one in their ultimate evidence.

With all their brilliance the Greeks made slight progress in the knowledge of the universe. Aristotle sometimes approached our modern inductive methods, but for ages the world was beguiled from them by the imaginations of Plato. In his *Phædon*

he taught that to attain truth we must suppress
sense. With him phenomena were illusions. Only in
the soul itself must we seek those eternal types which
are verities. This turned man into himself for the
images of truth. His physical nature was depre-
ciated to exalt the intellectual. For facts and laws
he found the illusions he sought to escape.

Modern Science secures her triumphs by regard-
ing man in his whole constitution. She employs the
senses to help the intellect. On facts she bases her
eternal structure. Her astronomy she verifies by
her telescope. By her spectroscope she proves to
the eye the unity of the universe. Chemistry in re-
tort and battery employs touch and taste and smell.
Geology, botany, mineralogy, and a whole sister-
hood of studies base themselves on observation.
Modern Science bears into the midnight of nature
the lamp of sense that she may guide reason to the
laws of the universe.

How with Scripture? Consider Prophecy! Does
she employ abstract processes, metaphysical deductions, and philosophical speculations? Like Science, she appeals to sense. In Isaiah, in Jeremiah,
in Ezekiel, study the pictures of Babylon and Nineveh and Tyre and Petra and Jerusalem! Pass from
the predictions of the Scripture to the descriptions
of the explorer! The sketch of the seer corresponds
to the narrative of the traveler. On the page of Revelation the eye reads the prophecy, and on the page
of Providence the eye reads the fulfillment. More
striking still the relations between the graphic de-

lineations of the Messiah in the Old Testament and the vivid histories of the Messiah in the New Testament. From creation to judgment scriptural prophecy, like physical science, is an appeal to the eye.

Nor is it different with miracles! Would the Creator to a rude people evince his personality? He the invisible makes himself seen. He the inaudible makes himself heard. Revealed only to man's soul, he would be confounded with man's soul. Therefore he exhibits himself to man's sense. He breaks the uniformity of nature that lulls into pantheistic stupor, and interferes with the mechanism of his universe whose very perfection is an opiate to faith. From his repose he comes forth in his majesty to convince of his existence and impress the obligation of his laws, not by arguments to reason, but by displays to eye and ear. His attributes are no longer unrespected as when slumbering in his Godhead. They become awful and impressive facts incorporated with the world's history and perpetual reminders to humanity. Or is an ideal of virtue to be displayed? It is not by the song of the poet, the picture of the artist, the eloquence of the orator, or the speculation of the philosopher, but in the birth and deeds and death of a visible and audible man. In Jesus wisdom is a life. The symbols of his love are a manger and a cross. With him immortality is not an argument, but a resurrection, and not an expectation, but a fact.

In appeals to sense Scripture and Science agree.

Ancient Philosophy scorned the physical in man.
Hence she gave no progress to humanity. Everything petrified under her touch until Bacon, following the hints of Aristotle, opened to our race the
true path to a knowledge of the laws of the universe.
Based on observation and experiment, Science became a power. Through the body she marries the
soul to nature, and at once a new birth for our race
of light and bliss and glory. But long before Science Religion had pursued a similar method. Always to eye and ear her miracles and prophecies
had been evidences. *Science and Christianity, in
their proofs, to reason, rest alike on the senses.*
How strong, then, the presumption that they are
parts of the same scheme and derived from the same
original!

## XII

### HYPERCRITICISM AND CREATION

We have seen that Hypercriticism leads logically to the conclusion that Genesis is an incredible forgery. It represents the first chapter of the Bible as a poetic legend, and not an historical narration. I propose to show that theological extremists obliterate from Scripture a record which modern science proves could come only from inspiration.

Latitude is in the very genius of the Hebrew word יוֹם, *yōm*, translated *day*. Without reference to duration *light* is called *day*. Evening and morning together make *day*. Yet, ruled by the sun, only *part* of twenty-four hours means *day*, while in the second chapter of Genesis *day* includes the whole period of creation. We can then adjust the ancient Hebrew word to our modern discovery, and without strain denominate it an indefinite *cycle*.

Let us now examine the Mosaic history in the light of nineteenth century science! Our telescopes disclose boundless tracts of vaporous matter diffused through the infinitudes of the universe. These nebulæ are now believed to be the primal elements of creation—the original materials of all worlds—the illimitable storehouses from which elaborate stars and suns and systems. Yet in the seventh verse of the first chapter of Genesis, as in other parts of Scripture, the Hebrew מַיִם means *clouds,* which answers precisely to the Latin word used by science. "In the beginning God created the heavens and the earth." Here we have expressed the omnipotent volition bringing into existence those *nebulæ* which are the constituents of the universe. Over these brooded the divine Spirit breathing into elements the potencies and possibilities of all future worlds.

Science teaches that space is pervaded by a subtle luminiferous ether whose waves impinging on the eye make vision. This was created by the almighty fiat of the FIRST DAY. Then we are told that rotations of nebulæ throwing off worlds developed heat. By brilliant revolving spheres around a blazing sun our system was illuminated. A sublime cycle of light!

Nor does science suggest a less satisfactory explanation of the SECOND DAY.

The Greek *stereoma,* and the Latin *firmamentum,* and the English *firmament* improperly translate the Hebrew *rākia*, which does not imply solidity, but simply means *expanse.* With scientific accuracy the scriptural word describes the atmosphere. For ages our earth was a surging volcanic ocean revolving as a sphere of flame. Out of its wild and universal fires was slowly elaborated our air. The SECOND DAY was thus a cycle of atmospheric development. What infinite wisdom in the work! Air enfolds earth with a maternal mantle. To vegetables and animals innumerable it is the breath of life. It feeds, too, the fires necessary for human existence and comfort. In it are born the clouds, without which earth would be a sterile and inanimate waste. Elaborations of, perhaps, billions of years resulted in nice chemical proportions which, slightly changed, would make our air a poison causing universal death.

Science tells us that after a cycle of fire over earth succeeded a cycle of water. An ocean covered our globe. Beneath its surface worked mighty volcanic forces. Amid smoke and flame and earthquake-thunders, mountain-islands were heaved above the deep. Continents were born. During this THIRD DAY Asia and Africa and America and Australia took the shapes familiar on our maps. Alps and Andes and Himalayas piled themselves into the sky. Hills and valleys and islands were formed to diversify the world. Seas and lakes and brooks and rivers prepared their channels, and oceans became bounded by their shores. Grasses were created to robe earth with everlasting green. Trees appear indispensable to humanity—the oak, the pine, the cedar, needed for fuel and structure, with those which bear the delicious pear, the luscious plum, the exquisite peach, the healthful apple, the grape, the melon, the nut, with other innumerable productions of forest and orchard and vineyard, having in themselves the mysterious power of perpetual propagation. While this wonderful vegetable life is preparing for far-future use volcanic fires are fusing many necessary substances. In the joints and fissures of rocks smelt metals without which civilization would be impossible. Gems also shape to flash and glitter in their peerless glory. It is science that reveals to us all this provident wisdom Hypercriticism would obliterate from our Bibles. Our present convenience and culture we trace to ancient cycles described in Genesis. Our wheat draws into its stalks nutriments stored in earth when there was no sign of a

11

future tiller. The leaf owes its verdure, the flower its bloom, the fruit its flavor, and the grain its nourishment to soils formed amid changes of ocean and continent which terminated ages previous to the planned result. Our iron and zinc and lead and copper and all other metals of manufacture and commerce, the gold and the silver that circulate in our currency, the gems sparkling on the brow of beauty and flashing from the crowns of kings, were shaped by flames under mountain pressure when and where they had no perceptible value, and brought from their darkness, after cycles, by man for his convenience, to be visible proofs of a sovereign wisdom which Hypercriticism obscures when it converts the Mosaic record of creation into mythical legendary poetry.

By land and by sea the volcanic commotions of ages filled our atmosphere with mist and smoke. While invisible the celestial bodies could not rule day and night, and shine as signs and determine seasons. But a time arrives when vapors no longer obscure the sky. The curtains of the cycles are lifted. Sun and moon and stars appear in their daily and nightly courses, at first dimly and occasionally, but finally as we now behold in their order and glory. Cycles of astronomical and chemical and geographical change have terminated in the sublime FOURTH DAY. Around the sun as a center revolve the planets with their circling moons. Light flashing millions of miles is exquisitely adapted to billions of eyes whose vision may extend from a point to a universe. Each blade of grass is provided.

On meadow and mountain the little wild flower receives its portion. Not an insect glittering in a sunbeam that is not made glad by what it needs. Animals and vegetables innumerable draw life from the inexhaustible sun, shining without waste and flooding earth with joy and glory. Divine the infinite exactitude! Days and years, signs and seasons, marked with mathematical precision! You can express their laws and returns in algebraic formulas. The solar system is a clock. Our watches we regulate by the sun and our chronometers by the stars. Affairs of home and business we arrange according to the mathematics and mechanics of the heavens.

Vegetable life began in simple grasses. Although we cannot prove evolution, we remark *progress* from the humbler to the superior complex forms. Each cycle is a development from the dimness of evening to the brightness of morning. But as yet no intelligence and no volition! What a stupendous advance in the instinct and will of even a primal mollusk! Wise and wonderful in its ascent the work of the FIFTH and the SIXTH DAYS! Earth and air and ocean swarm with creatures which can swim and fly and run and walk, using their souls and bodies for preservation and happiness, and endowed with organs to perpetuate species without intermixture and confusion down through the cycles of time to the end of the earth. Last of all and lord of all and crown of all and glory of all, man appears in the image of his Almighty Maker.

## XIII

### HYPERCRITICISM AND PROPHECY

THE most subtle and dangerous attack on Christianity is against its evidences. Prophecy and miracle are appointed proofs. Undermine these pillars, and you overthrow the edifice. Style Revelation a literature! By a word you have reduced the divine to the human. Moses! Elijah! Isaiah! Did they declare a future known only to Omniscience and communicated by Jehovah, or were they mere men of genius like Shakespeare and Milton and Goethe? If the latter, then were the apostles also *literati*. Ministers of the Gospel are lecturers to please men, and not ambassadors called and authorized to proclaim the salvation of God.

We hold that Incarnation is the key to Scripture. All its evidences center in this sublimest fact of the universe, and can be interpreted only in its light. Hence our difficulty in convincing skeptics who scorn the sole clew to Revelation. Nor can we always reason from the originals of Scripture in the inspired words of God. Manuscripts have been corrupted, and translations are in the language of man. But the prophecies we are to cite are the same in all versions, and bear in themselves and fulfillments the indubitable proofs of a divine veracity. Having the substance, the form is not indispensable. However necessary the shell and the casket, yet the treasure is the kernel and the jewel.

Hypercriticism overlooks the preparation of the

prophet. Moses and Paul were called by God. But they surpassed all mortals in natural genius and laborious education for their work. To place on their thrones inferior men is to minimize the gifts of heaven. By primal endowment and protracted discipline both were brought into harmony with the divine Spirit. The more perfect the human instrument the less apparent the celestial impulse. Seeking gold and glory, Balaam was enslaved to himself and constrained by Omniscience, while Paul and Moses, inspired, were yet at liberty.

Impressions of miracles are greatest in the present. Time casts a mist over memory. Does prophecy anticipate and record the grandest facts of history down to the end of time, and confirm Revelation with immortal proofs, and foreshadow eternity itself? These questions can only be answered by the fulfillment of the scriptural predictions. Of these we can here select but a few as specimens of the whole. The inquiry is fundamental. Prophecy connects itself with the Old Testament, and is made the foundation of the New. If we succeed in our task, we show that in discrediting Moses and David and Isaiah and Daniel, and the other venerable seers, Hypercriticism resembles that infatuation which would pull down the stars and overturn the foundations of the universe. However, we must leave to others the verdict on our work.

### Noah's Grand Prophecy.

Yes! We turn first to that Genesis Hypercriticism would tear to fragments. In such a mine we

seek a celestial gem, which resembles the diamond
treasuring the glory of God amid its terrestrial
darkness.

Scripture describes Noah as the man who received
the promise, built the ark, survived the flood, saw
the bow in the cloud, heard Jehovah's covenanting
voice, and became second head of the human race.
Overcome by a mortal infirmity, out of his humiliation flashed a prophecy having the seal of Omniscience, because it is a visible epitome of the future
of the world:

"Cursed be Canaan; a servant of servants shall
he be unto his brethren. Blessed be the Lord God
of Shem; and Canaan shall be his servant. God
shall enlarge Japheth, and he shall dwell in the tents
of Shem; and Canaan shall be his servant."

## HAM.

To punish the impiety of the youngest son the
Almighty revealed to him the servile degradation
of his descendants. These made their home in Palestine and Phœnicia. Fair and fertile Canaan became notorious for its idolatries and immoralities.
Over its incorrigible people Jehovah pronounced
sentence of extermination. A nation of Egyptian
slaves was called and trained to execute his sovereign purpose and fulfill his omniscient prediction.
Under Joshua the liberated Israelites became conquerors, swept over Canaan, defeated giants, seized
cities, possessed the land, and subjected the people.
Sometimes, indeed, the victors, seduced by idol-

aters, were themselves vanquished. But in each
extremity arose heroic deliverers. Five hundred
years after Moses David won his crown, and ex-
pelled from Jerusalem the Jebusites, who were the
last remnants of the ancient Hamites. What Joshua
began was ended by Solomon, and to Shem became
Canaan a "servant of servants." Chronicles records:

"As for all the people that were left of the Hit-
tites, and the Amorites, and the Perizzites, and the
Hivites, and the Jebusites, which were not of Israel,
but of their children, who were left after them in the
land, whom the children of Israel consumed not,
them did Solomon make to pay tribute until this
day."

We presume that Scripture may be accepted by
Hypercriticism as a reliable record of facts where
we have no other authority. But, if we are mistaken, we will now turn to profane history, which
will be less liable to dispute.

## JAPHETH.

"God shall *enlarge* Japheth." The Hebrew root
of Japheth signifies to *enlarge*. Thus *enlarge* is in
the name and in the prediction. And history confirms prophecy. Nineveh and Babylon were the
two grand centers of ancient Asian empire. Both
cities were founded by Hamites. But these vast
swarming capitals, with their populous territories,
were soon conquered and governed by the descendants of Japheth. From Japheth, too, the Lydians,

Medes, and Persians. Japheth, also, was the father
of the Greeks, who colonized the shores and islands
of the Mediterranean, and under Alexander extended
their dominion over the greatest part of the civilized world. And from Japheth the Romans,
who carved by the sword a yet wider empire. The
Tartar hordes who have swarmed into Europe, the
populations of India, Japan, and China, half the
world's inhabitants, sprang from Japheth. Canada!
Australia! Our American republic! All claim
Japheth as their ancestor. Both the Eastern and
Western continents have thus been mostly enlarged
by Japheth, who has peopled the British empire.
Asia, Europe, America, Atlantic and Pacific isles,
have furnished billions of witnesses to the truth of a
prophecy imbedded in a book which hypercritics
must believe a forgery.

## Shem.

"Blessed be the Lord God of Shem!" Noah
overflows with gratitude for signal favors to Shem,
whose descendants in Abraham received the Messianic covenant-promise, and among whom was the
abode of Jehovah in the glory of the Shekinah.
Japheth, also, was "to dwell in the tents of
Shem." Jews gathered to themselves Christians. Each Old Testament prophet and New
Testament apostle was a Jew. Messiah was a Jew.
Paul, the great Gentile teacher, was a Jew. Possibly excepting Job, not a book in our Bible written
save by a Jew. The Christian Church is composed

of the sons of Japheth who dwell in the tents of
Shem, the father of the Jew.  Our world testifies to
the verity of a prediction delivered just after the
deluge.

## ISHMAEL.

Two nations derived from Abraham have power-
fully impressed humanity.  One has been a com-
mercial, and the other a military, people.  Both,
subjects of most vivid prophecies, now mingle with
the greatest movements of our world.

Speaking to fugitive Hagar, despairing in the
wilderness, Jehovah said:

"Thou shalt bear a son and shall call his name
Ishmael.  He will be a wild ass man.  His hand shall
be against every man, and every man's hand shall be
against him, and he shall dwell in the presence of
his brethren."

What a picture of Ishmael—painting, too, his pos-
terity!  Arabs resemble the wild ass.  They love
the wilderness.  They scorn the city.  They range
desert and mountain.  In Arabia, Palestine, Assyria,
Africa, they live in perpetual war.  Rapine is their
occupation.  A visit by strangers to Mecca, their
capital, is almost inevitable death.  A caravan to
Petra or Jerusalem or Assyria must be protected
by soldiers from prowling Arabs, who are the thieves
of Egypt and the slave-dealers of the rest of Africa.
Vermin and hyenas are not so feared and detested.
Europe is now arrayed against these Ishmaelitish
traffickers in human flesh.  At this moment England
is fighting them in the Soudan.  Always and every-

where "their hand is against every man, and every man's hand is against them." Yet, as predicted, they "DWELL in the presence of their brethren." Hated by all, they survive all. They have never been subjugated. Chaldeans, Assyrians, Egyptians, attempted vainly their conquest. Cyrus subdued Media, subjected Lydia, took Babylon, and was baffled by Arabia. Alexander conquered the world, except Ishmael. Victor of earth, Rome failed in his desert. Here lived Mohammed, whose followers, like locust-clouds, swarmed forth to devour and destroy. They mastered western Asia. They subdued northern Africa. They enslaved the fairest region of Spain. Combining with the Turk, they threatened Europe and terrify the Sultan in Constantinople.

## ISRAEL.

Hypercriticism clouds Deuteronomy into forgery. Yet in this maligned book we have for all time the portrait and the history of the Jewish people. In the twenty-eighth chapter we read:

"Ye shall be plucked from the land. The Lord shall scatter thee among all people. Among these nations thou shalt find no ease. Thy life shall hang in doubt of thee. Thou shalt become an astonishment, a proverb, and a byword."

Shalmaneser fulfilled this Mosaic prediction. He took Samaria and transported its inhabitants. Then Sennacherib spoiled Judah. Nebuchadnezzar conquered the nation, burned Jerusalem, gave the plundered temple to the torch, and carried the noblest

of the Jews to Babylon. Alexander was another
tyrant-master. Rome completed what Assyria began. Again the temple was burned, the city destroyed, the people exiled and enslaved. Arabs succeed Romans. After Saracen the Turk, who now
rules Judea. For ages commerce and captivity have
scattered Israel over earth. The Jew is "an astonishment and a proverb and a byword." How contrary this to everything else in human nature! The
Greek we love for his immortal past. We see the
Italian in the halo of his Latin lineage and literature
and achievement. Each European shares the re-
nown of his illustrious ancestors. Yet what the
blessings to our race from Greece and Rome and
England compared with the salvation which comes
from the Jew! In him nature seems reversed, and
yet true to the prophetic picture. In proportion to
his blessing he is cursed. Yet, blasted, he is not to
be destroyed! For "when the fullness of the Gentiles shall come in, all Israel shall be saved." Oblit-
eration would falsify prediction. Like the mountain
bush, the Jew burns and is unconsumed. Mowed as
grass, he springs from ruin and rises immortal.
Dying, he lives. In both destruction and preservation proving Mosaic prophecy the Omniscience of
Jehovah.

## EGYPT.

The Blue and White Nile from the Abyssinian
mountains and equatorial lakes pour down the fer-
tilizing floods which have enriched the land of
Pharaohs. Their narrow valley nurtured the most

splendid of the ancient civilizations. No race has created a monument equaling the vast massive grandeur of the great pyramid. In architectural art the columned hall of Karnak stands supreme. A moonlight view of this temple is the most impressive scene amid the ruins of antiquity. In its forest of sculptured pillars genius has secured a triumph exceeding the grace of the Parthenon and the majesty of the Colosseum. Archæology now displays the whole life of Egypt pictured on her tombs, and the face of Rameses is as familiar as the features of Victoria. At this moment explorations are dissipating mythical mists, and giving us reliable chronology and history. English enterprise is erecting structures on the Nile which will make all seasons fertile in Egypt and surpass in blessing all ever accomplished in royal tombs, temples, and pyramids.

How vivid the coloring of Ezekiel in describing the glory of the land of the Nile! Like Assyria, Egypt is a cedar of Lebanon, growing toward heaven and sheltering its fowls. But after this picture of beauty a spectacle of ruin! "On the mountains and in the valleys his branches are broken and his boughs fallen." Such is the end of Pharaohs! Egypt, says Ezekiel, shall have *"no more a prince* in the land," "shall be the basest of kingdoms," and shall "exalt herself no more among the nations." Papyri and monuments inform us that seven centuries before Christ Esarhaddon invaded the Nile valley. His son Asshurbanipal resumed his father's work—seized cities and massacred inhabitants, boasting, "I left not one." Archæology confirms Josephus in his account of the conquests of Nebuchadnezzar. For forty years Egypt groaned under the Persian yoke imposed by Cambyses, monster son of the great Cyrus. The sword of Alexander gave their scepter to the debauched Ptolemies, whose dynasty was ended by the suicide of infamous Cleopatra. Roman domination followed; Octavius Cæsar reduced the realm of Rameses to a province. Egypt was tilled by slaves to feed her conquerors. Over her, six centuries after Augustus, Caliph Omar with his Saracens swept like locusts. He gave the Alexandrian library to the torch. Cruel Mamelukes succeeded with usurped authority. Their sultan was hanged in the sixteenth century by the Emperor Selim, and Egypt annexed to the Ottoman empire. She has been for twenty-five centuries, as Ezekiel predicted, "basest of kingdoms," has had no native monarch, and has no prospect of independence among nations.

Ismail Pasha seemed the deliverer of his country. He built railroads, erected manufactories, conquered the Soudan to the equator. Now, surely, Egypt will recover her ancient glory! No! A cloud soon darkens her morning sun! Ismail becomes bankrupt. He piles on Egypt a mountain of debt, and flies to die in exile. The Suez Canal, built by his money, passes to the control of England. Her rule is a perpetual blessing. Yet it is a *foreign* domination. British bayonets keep the khedive on the throne, and he pays tribute to Constantinople. Never before had Egypt so many masters.

## Nineveh.

On the opposite sides of Mount Niphates are born the Tigris and Euphrates to fertilize Mesopotamia. Along the banks of these rivers rose the cities which have given splendor to Assyria. Here Botta began explorations eclipsed by Layard. Above the Tigris stood Nineveh. On lofty brick platforms were erected her temples and palaces, yielding to modern enterprise the secrets of a mighty metropolis and histories of buried dynasties. Yet sculpture and painting have not shed most light on vast Mesopotamian cities. Cuneiform tablets and cylinders give more accurate and extensive information than the statues and pictures of temples and palaces. Burned clay survives papyrus and parchment, and affords the most durable form in which history has ever written her records. Little wedges, ingeniously arranged, preserve biographies of peoples and monarchs, tell us of the rise and fall of empires, reveal the glory and decay of dynasties. As the Rosetta Stone guided to the interpretation of Egyptian hieroglyphics, so the Behistun Rock gave us our knowledge of Assyrian characters.

The cuneiform records attest the Scriptural declarations. Nineveh sat queen of the Orient. In the graphic prophetic language this proud capital resembled a lofty tree, towering over mountain cliffs, and under its majestic shadow gathering the beasts of earth and the birds of heaven. Yet was to be shattered into irrecoverable ruin! Zephaniah wrote, He "will make Nineveh a desolation," and Nahum cried, "Woe to the bloody city! The fire shall devour thee, and the sword shall cut thee off."

Nineveh dropped like a sun from midheaven. Her glory culminated in Asshurbanipal. His son Asshuremitiln brought eclipse. Modern exploration supplies a reason. We have now proofs that Scythian hordes poured over Assyria. They most probably enfeebled the empire, paralyzed Nineveh, and led to her fall.

Saracus is the Asshuremitiln of the cuneiform cylinders. When he succeeded his illustrious father the throne of Media was occupied by Cyaxares, the legendary Arbaces. Aided by Nabopolassar, of Babylon, he advanced against Nineveh. The city became an easy prey to these combined enemies. Diodorus relates the catastrophe. While Saracus feasted the Median monarch came on him by surprise, slew his soldiers, mastered his camp, seized his metropolis. Nahum foretells that "the gates of the river should be opened, and the palace dissolved," and history records that the river overflowed and that the palace was burned.

After its overthrow a cloud settled over Nineveh. Her splendor was obscured in the growing glory of Babylon. As early as the second century Lucian said that no man knew where the city had stood. Within our own memory Mr. Layard discovered its melancholy ruins. How his book verifies the sacred oracles! The "heaps" of the prophet correspond to the "mounds" of the traveler. Nineveh is a "desolation." Piles of earth cover palaces of monarchs and temples of divinities. Owls hoot and jackals bark amid broken columns, shattered alabasters, and prostrate images which witness a vanished glory predicted and depicted in Scripture.

## BABYLON.

Babylon stood on both sides of the Euphrates. Our modern archæology displaces the glowing pictures of Herodotus. Yet discovery has not diminished our admiration for this most magnificent capital of the ancient world. Although the growth of centuries under conquering kings, Nebuchadnezzar crowned it with its brightest glory, which proved to be the splendor of a setting sun. The spoils of the world were brought into Babylon. Her lofty palaces were filled with paintings and statues and all the noblest works of Chaldean art. Overtopped by towers, adorned by gates of glittering brass, her walls were unrivaled. The gold flashing from the roof of Belus was higher than the great pyramid. Nebuchadnezzar's gardens were the marvels of antiquity. Cities, kingdoms, empires, contributed their captured treasures to enrich and beautify this peerless imperial metropolis. Babylon became the prophetic type of successful earthly domination. She was the "golden city," the "lady of kingdoms," the "beauty and glory of the Chaldee's excellency," the impurpled queen of the world whose scepter ruled and whose cup intoxicated the nations.

We will not here repeat the accounts given by Herodotus and Xenophon of the youth and education and conquests of the great Cyrus. They are beautiful literary mosaics composed of fancy, myth, and history. Most probably, as represented, the Persian victor drained the river, entered over its bed, passed through the opened gates, slew the reveling people, killed the feasting king, and seized his crown and capital. An inscription by Cyrus, recently deciphered, does not state how the city was taken. But a victor of Media and Lydia in brilliant battles would not wish to perpetuate the memory of a *stratagem* by which he took Babylon. An oriental conqueror recorded only what added to his glory. It was *possession* of the Chaldean metropolis which crowned the career of Cyrus.

Nor will we pause here to discuss that Hypercriticism which from its archæological nebulæ draws its infallible conclusions, and turns fulfillments of prophecies into proofs that they were written after the events they profess to predict. We will simply state predictions which all may read in the light of the discoveries of our century. Mr. Layard restored to the world the knowledge of the grand capital of Nebuchadnezzar, and his vivid descriptions are the best commentaries on the accuracy of the biblical delineations:

"I will dry up the rivers. Cyrus shall perform all my pleasure. I will open the two-leaved gates. I will give thee the treasures of darkness. I, the Lord, which call thee by name, am the Lord God of Israel. How hast thou fallen from heaven. O Lucifer, son of morning! Thou saidst, I will exalt my

12

throne above the stars of God; yet thou shalt be brought down to hell. I will stir up the Medes and Persians. Babylon shall become heaps; wild beasts of the island shall dwell there and owls; it shall be no more inhabited forever."

## DANIEL'S IMAGE.

This is not the place to defend Daniel. Christ calls him "*the* prophet." Jews believe him a prophet. The Christian Church canonizes him a prophet. From mistakes of copyists and translators Hypercriticism makes the book of Daniel not a prophecy, but a fabrication. Let me simply state one of its marvelous predictions with the fulfillments!

Under threat of death, summoned by Nebuchadnezzar, Daniel explained to that tyrant-monarch the IMAGE seen in his dream.

1. "Thou," said the prophet, "art the head of gold."

Nebuchadnezzar was the creator of his dynasty, the conqueror of kingdoms, the most illustrious monarch-builder. The glory of his imperial diadem outdazzled the splendors of all his predecessors. He had conquered Asia from the Nile to the Ganges, and ruled the Orient with unexampled power and magnificence. Aptly he was styled "Head of gold."

2. "After thee shall arise another kingdom inferior to thee," which Daniel compares to the "breast and arms of silver" of an image.

The career of Cyrus was more brilliant than that of Nebuchadnezzar. With his Persians, victorious over Medes and Lydians, his united armies took Babylon. Yet was his dynasty a descent from gold to silver. Nebuchadnezzar *created* the glory of empire and metropolis which Cyrus *wrested,* not from himself, but his degenerate and dissolute and blaspheming grandson, Belshazzar. The monster Cambyses succeeded his father to end the Persian line. Gaining the throne by artifice and murder, Darius proved a wise monarch. After him came the luxurious and capricious Xerxes, whose vast hosts were repelled by Greece. Disgraced and enfeebled by its monarchs, the Medo-Persian dynasty perished in infamy.

3. "His belly and thighs of brass," said Daniel; and explained, "another third kingdom of brass shall rule over the earth."

So it occurred! Alexander conquered Asia. How striking the prophetic word describing his dominion! Brass glittered in the armor of the Greeks. Yet an alloy! Fit emblem of mingled Hellenes and barbarians! And inferior to silver and gold! Always the empire of Alexander was covered with a cloud of doubt from his ungovernable passions. It was divided after his miserable death among his four generals and lost its Grecian character. In Europe it became feeble, in Asia distracted, and in Africa detestable under the loathsome Ptolemies, whose shame terminated in Cleopatra.

4. "And the fourth kingdom shall be strong as iron. As the toes of the feet were part of iron and part of clay, so shall the kingdom be partly strong

and partly broken. Whereas thou sawest iron mixed with clay, they shall not mingle themselves with the seed of man, even as iron is not mixed with clay."

After the Macedonian empire the Roman! How perfect the quaint word-picture of Daniel! Iron represents the discipline and valor of Rome by which she ruled the world. It is the metal, too, of peace as well as of war. From it not only spade and plow, but sword and javelin. And Rome secured in peace what she won by battle. Yet the iron was mixed with clay! And in the *feet* which support the body! Forever in Rome the plebeian and patrician were in contest! Mass against class! Conquerors without were enemies within! Symbol complete of a divided and yet victorious people! On the skirts of the empire always watching and vengeful barbarians! Down into their vile earth sank the imperial magnificence of Rome! Her eagles seized and defiled by savage hordes! Gaul! Goth! Hun! Vandal! Their brutal armies brought the ignominious ruin!

5. "And in the days of these kings shall the God of heaven set up a kingdom which shall never be destroyed. Forasmuch as thou sawest that the stone was cut out of the mountain without hands, and that it breaks in pieces the iron, and the brass, the clay, the silver, and gold, the great God hath made known to the king what shall come to pass."

Each previous empire founded by force had perished by force. Only universal love can make everlasting dominion. Without hands this last immortal dynasty! Not, then, established by human agency, but the power of God! Its Messiah a carpenter! Its instruments fishermen and publicans! Its symbols a dove, a lamb, a cross! Its power—the Holy Ghost! Before our eyes the words of Daniel are proving him an inspired prophet! Everywhere Christian civilization triumphing! The stone becoming a mountain that will surely fill the world!

## THE PROPHET LIKE MOSES.

Jehovah walked and talked in paradise when he communicated his first prophecy. Jehovah "spake unto Noah" when he commanded the ark, and declared the covenant. Jehovah revealed himself to Abraham in a vision; to Jacob in a dream; to Isaiah and Ezekiel in a visible glory; to Jeremiah in words; and to Daniel by an angel. But transcending all were his communications to Moses. On Sinai he saw and heard the God of Israel, and spake to him "face to face" before the shekinah and under the cloud of the tabernacle. And in this full, direct, and familiar communication from the Father Christ chiefly resembles Moses. Yet, while typifying two opposite dispensations, it is wonderful in how many minor ways the one pictures the other without forced or fantastic interpretation. Quoting from Deuteronomy, Stephen says, in the words of Moses, "The Lord thy God will raise thee up a Prophet from the midst of thy brethren, *like unto me;* unto him shall ye hearken."

Moses was a prophet; so was Christ. Moses was a ruler; so was Christ. Moses was a teacher; so was Christ. Moses fled from King Pharaoh, and Christ from King Herod. Both were in Egypt. A cloud led Moses through the sea; a cloud covered him on Sinai; a cloud guided him in the wilderness; and a cloud was over Jesus at his baptism, transfiguration, and ascension. Moses rescued from Egyptian superstition, and Christ from Satanic darkness. Moses broke the chain of a tyrant, and Christ rends the fetter of sin. On a mountain Moses received the Law, and on a mountain Christ declared his Gospel. Each by miracle sealed his message. Moses fasted forty days, and forty days fasted Christ. Moses supplied manna in the wilderness, and Christ bread in the desert. Moses refused honor from a king, and Christ the honor of a king. Moses triumphed over magicians, and Christ over demons. On twelve tribes Moses founded his government, and on twelve apostles Christ his Church. Moses constituted seventy elders, and Christ appointed seventy disciples. Moses walked through the sea, and Christ over the sea. Moses from the rock brought natural waters, and Christ from himself gives spiritual waters. When descending the mountain shone the face of Moses, and the face of Christ when transfigured on the mountain. The hands of Moses were held up for victory over Amalek, and the hands of Christ were stretched on the cross for triumph over Satan. Moses instituted, and Christ spiritualized, the passover. With typical blood Moses ratified the old

covenant, and with his own blood Christ the new.
Moses brought darkness over Egypt, and Christ
over Judea.  Moses lifted up the serpent, and Christ
was lifted up on the cross.  Moses and Christ appeared together in the dazzling splendor of the
transfiguration, and are united in the apocalyptic
song of the celestial glory.

## JERUSALEM.

Our Saviour sat on Olivet and looked down over
Jerusalem.  Before him stood the temple in unrivaled grace and grandeur.  Its silver and gold
dazzled in the morning sun.  Josephus describes it
as a mountain of splendor.  On its terrace of enormous stones it towered over the valleys below sublime in its seeming indestructibility.  The Jews had
now accepted the Roman yoke and trusted in the
imperial armies.  Over their temple was the shield
of the invincible emperor who ruled earth on the
banks of the Tiber.  Yet the Omniscient eye of the
Master pierced the future, and his lips proclaimed
the inevitable ruin.  He said:

1. "Many shall come in my name, saying, I am
Christ, and shall deceive many."

Soon after our Saviour's death Simon Magus "be-
witched the people."  Dositheus, the Samaritan,
claimed to be the Messiah.  When Claudius wore the
purple Theudas promised to divide Jordan, but was
captured and decapitated.  While Nero was on the
throne impostors calling themselves Christs were
killed daily, and yet deceived multitudes.

2. Previous to the overthrow of Jerusalem our Saviour foretold "wars," "rumors," "famines," "pestilences," and "earthquakes."

Josephus records the facts which fulfill these predictions. Caligula ordered his statue to be erected in the temple. Judea was in such commotion that tillage was neglected. Dissensions, insurrections, and slaughters marked the reigns of Claudius and Nero. "Nation rose against nation." Jews and Syrians slew each other. In Scythopolis, Alexandria, and Damascus thousands perished. Palestine was a scene of blood. Civil wars burst out in Italy. Famines and pestilences and earthquakes destroyed and desolated. The historian says that men thought the universe to be confounded.

3. There were to be fearful "sights" and "signs." We need not here repeat the prodigies recorded by Josephus—portents in heaven and on earth which terrified the nations and filled the Jews with ominous dread.

4. "Great tribulation," our Saviour predicted, "such as was not from the beginning of the world." Here again Josephus is witness. While the Romans without carried forward the siege amid furious battles, within three parties of Jews fought each other like wild beasts, robbing and murdering. Internal war was more destructive than the imperial army. Mad citizens burned their own magazines and reduced themselves to starvation. Famine drove to despair. Hungry men snatched food from perishing women and children. One frenzied mother

slew and ate her own son. Pentecost had crowded Jerusalem with strangers, and a million perished in the siege. The pages of Josephus recording these horrors are the most ghastly in human history.

5. Our Saviour also predicted that the temple would be destroyed and Jerusalem left desolate. Only after incredible difficulties could Titus take the city. He implored the Jews to save their capital by submission. They scorned the imperial mercy. Against the emperor's orders a furious soldier hurled a torch into the temple. Flames burst forth, and the edifice was a ruin. Titus then ordered the city to destruction, and its whole history since has been a fulfillment of the prophecies of Christ.

## MESSIAH.

Recently in Palestine two ladies found fragments of Apocryphal Ecclesiasticus in Hebrew. By search in the Genizah of Cairo, the Bodleian Library, and the British Museum, missing chapters have been recovered, and the greater part of the book restored. More than two thousand years have elapsed since it was written. That its fragments, separated for centuries, should have been found in four different parts of the earth, to be reunited, might well have been pronounced impossible. Had we read on one of the pages a prediction of this result by the scribe, we must have believed his foresight miraculous. No human mind by itself could have thus pierced the future, overcoming improbabilities from four cities in three continents. Yet in the case of the Messiah, from Moses to Malachi, including a thousand years, are scores of Old Testament symbols and prophecies meeting in Christ, and none else, and which, on a mathematical calculation of chances, compel us to the conclusion that not man, but God, was the Omniscient Author of this otherwise inexplicable foresight down through the vicissitudes of our mortal history.

We cannot here pause to show how the predictions of the Law are verified by the facts of the Gospel. In each detail of time and birth and life and death and resurrection and ascension the biography of Jesus Christ is a finished picture completing the outlines of beauty and glory penciled, especially, by Moses and David and Isaiah and Daniel. With a wider question we propose to occupy the remainder of this chapter.

Hypercriticism we now know by five sure marks: 1. It denies to Moses the authorship of the Pentateuch. 2. It considers the Jewish institutions not, as in Scripture, communications from Jehovah in the wilderness, but as natural developments in Canaan. 3. It affirms that the Holy Spirit could not give inerrant revelations to man. 4. It describes the apostolic Pentecostal witnesses as "frenzied" and "unintelligible" babblers. 5. It regards the Bible, not as a Revelation, but a Literature, and its prophets, not as inspired by the Holy Ghost, but as writing under the mere impulses of human genius. By such views, less than a quarter of a century since, Ingersoll startled and shocked the Christian world.

Toward *him,* then, Hypercriticism is making its boasted progress. To eliminate the supernatural, and *thus* reconcile to the Bible, we now see to be its end and aim. Let us look to the book itself! It begins by declaring that God made the universe. In paradise Jehovah utters a prophecy with promise. From this glimmering point predictions brighten through ages into the Sun of Righteousness. Prophecies, like stars, shine in every book of the Old Testament. Called by Jehovah, its writers, in the name of Jehovah, declare the words of Jehovah. They profess to reveal the future of cities, kingdoms, nations, empires, races. The New Testament concludes the scheme begun in the Old. By their *fulfillment* prophecies are to verify a Redemption, predestined from eternity, to offer man remission of sin through faith in the blood of Jesus, his Brother and Incarnate God, and by the power of the Holy Spirit promised to abide in the Church for the salvation of the world. Beyond time are revealed resurrection and judgment and heaven. The supernatural of the Almighty in redemption harmonizing with himself in creation and providence.

Could human genius unfold the history of the world? Were Hebrew prophets liars, with no more inspiration than Homers and Platos and Virgils and Ciceros and Dantes and Miltons? And are their predictions not, as declared in Scripture, from the Holy Ghost, but deceptive guesses of presuming mortals? On the prophets Jesus founded his Messiahship. He fulfilled the prophets, quoted the

prophets, sanctioned the prophets. Apostles appeal
to prophets as supreme and unquestionable authority. Yet, with infidelity, Hypercriticism undermines
the prophets on whom Christianity is based. Its
emissaries are seminary professors vowed and paid
to defend the Word of God. They style the Bible,
not a Revelation, but a Literature. Can a Literature
predict the future? Can a Literature remit sin?
Can a Literature bestow the Holy Ghost? Can a
Literature open paradise? Can a Literature raise
the dead, sit in judgment, create anew the heavens
and the earth, and determine everlasting awards?
Yet Literature is now the gospel of pulpits filled by
men educated and salaried to preach redemption.
What would hypercritics think of an ancient priest
who admired the temple's art and rejected the temple's worship? Jehovah made his house, not chiefly
for beauty, but salvation. He would regard as a
traitor the man receiving its revenues who should
deface its glory, deny its shekinah, and seek to exile
its Almighty Maker.

## XIV

### CHRIST

In his humanity Jesus Christ was an unlettered
Jew. While described with royal blood in his veins,
he was yet the reputed son of a poor mechanic. He
passed his early life in a small village. Rabbis were
not his instructors; publicans, fishermen, and arti-
sans were his companions. Indeed, for this very
reason his claim as a teacher was despised and rejected by the learned and exclusive doctors of Israel.
About the temple the priests met him with insults.
He had none of those advantages of culture in a
capital which polish style and enlarge intellect,
and are therefore essential to the highest literary
success.

Under the circumstances of his birth, occupation,
and associations we might expect something in the
thought and style of our Saviour indicating his
origin. You look for this in vain in the actions and
discourses of Jesus Christ. No instance can be produced of his provincialism, or vulgarity, or national
prejudice, or social jealousy, or offensive assump-
tion. Through his words and deeds breathes an
exquisite delicacy. Had this son of the people been
educated in a palace like that of his royal ancestors
David and Solomon, surrounded by princes, and
habituated to the elegances of a court, he could not
have manifested a more refined courtesy. If in
birth a peasant, he was in majesty a king. Nor
could a doctor about the temple have equaled this

obscure villager in literary merit. Nazareth out-shone Jerusalem. His parables, his sermons, his conversations exhibit what simplicity, what propri-ety, what aptness, what dignity! Style, argument, construction, are faultless. No literature, ancient or modern, has attained the point, beauty, and suc-cess of the discourses of Jesus. They are adapted to all ages, races, nationalities, individuals—to uni-versal man. Art is exceeded. The ideal of culture is realized and surpassed. Recall the Sermon on the Mount, the Prodigal Son, the Good Samaritan, the Wise and Foolish Virgins, Dives and Lazarus, the Great Supper, the Ten Talents! How exquisite the beauty of conception and expression! What genius of any era will suggest an improvement in thought, or word, or structure? Nothing of the provincial mechanic! Like the sun in a translucent drop, shines a glory visible without mortal blot. Je-sus was an uneducated Jew. Yet in no literature has been approached the touching and affectionate solemnity of the discourses before the crucifixion, the utterances after the resurrection, the majesty of command and promise previous to the ascension, or the sublimities of the descriptions of the judgment with its awards of life and death everlasting.

What could we hope from the nationality of Christ? He was a typical Jew. A descendant of Abraham, Isaac, and Jacob, of the tribe of Judah and the family of David, in his veins was the purest blood of his race. Nothing could be expected of him but the bigoted exclusiveness which marked the

Israelite. Moreover, in the forming period of his youth rabbinism was peculiarly dominant and restrictive. Its caste was narrow, remorseless, and malignant as that of India. The Jewish doctor despised the people. To touch the human herd was almost pollution. The Gentiles were to Jews outcast wretches excluded from Jehovah's covenant and doomed to everlasting exile from heaven. Barriers deep as hell separated all other nations from Israel. Out of such narrow social and political prejudice and passion how could spring a religion for humanity? Yet Jesus, a Jew of humble birth, education, and occupation, mounts above the prejudices of race and rabbi, above the creed of his parents, above the influences of his life, cuts through the iron network of caste, hurls down the walls of sect, rises superior to himself and his nation, and soars beyond all obstacles to the summit of an unsurpassable philanthropy, embracing the world. He announces a moral system of universal and eternal truth, whose doctrine of love is suitable to men and angels, and all intelligences who can ever owe allegiance to the throne of the Creator. And his life exemplified his doctrine. Truth from him shines a fit halo round the brow of the Messiah. It predisposes to belief in his claim as Lawgiver, Teacher, and Redeemer of humanity.

If with aims the most revolutionary Christ swept Judaism away, yet with a delicate conservatism he also perpetuated whatever was universal in application and everlasting in importance. In him who claimed to be Head of our race was minutely realized all national expectation. The ceremonial, the political, the moral of the Jewish old were amplified and glorified in the Christian new. Heaven and earth will pass away, but law and prophet have eternal fulfillment and enlargement in Jesus. Is this the spirit of imposture? Is this the temper of fanaticism? Is this conservatism compatible with fraud or folly? Greedy or ambitious human ignorance could never have contrived the minute, the varied, the innumerable correspondences between the types and promises and predictions of the Old Testament and the Messiah of the New Testament. Or if the loftiest mortal genius could have conceived so many exquisite, subtle, and beautiful harmonies, no possible earthly wisdom could have realized them in an actual life. Judaism was not so much abolished as perfected by its expansion into Christianity. In seeming destruction was full completion. The carnal becomes the spiritual; the particular the universal; the temporary the eternal. Germs reposing in a dead past flowered forth into a fresh life of everlasting beauty and glory. Now, this prudence, this commingling of opposites, this dignified reserve with daring courage, this revolutionary conservatism, are grand characteristics of Jesus Christ, and separate him forever from vulgar imposture.

History gives the key to the success of sages and heroes. Each rises as he typifies the genius of his nation. Confucius symbolizes China, and Buddha India. Alexander breathed the conquering spirit of Greece. Cæsar impersonated the democratic imperialism of Rome. Napoleon was incarnate France. Each beyond his own air and soil would have attained no brilliant success. Not one could have founded institutions for humanity. Mohammed for years was a mixture of Jew and Christian. But he was a failure and a fugitive. Now he drops his foreign cant and garb. The Arab in him bursts forth. He plans plunder by treachery and assassination. He murders his own tribe. He proclaims his creed by sword, and rewards victory by houris in paradise. Those desert marauders recognize the Arab of Arabs; in Mohammed they see their race ideal, and accept faith with fight. They rush to his standard, die for his creed, and bear the crescent of battle through Asia and Africa into Europe, menacing the world, yet failing, because they typified the genius of Arabia instead of the brotherhood of man. Differing from successful national heroes, Jesus impersonates Humanity.

The dream of the Jew was a Deliverer who would break the Roman chain, and establish in Jerusalem over the world the throne of David. Only such a Messiah could he see in the splendid visions of his prophets. His soul glowed with the hope of universal dominion conquered by the sword. Yet dazzled with such visions, a midnight was over the Jew. Roman soldiers held his capital and desecrated his temple. Everywhere over his city imperial eagles testified his disgraceful bondage. His passionate prayer was for a hero who in battle would break the

13

fetters of the chosen of Jehovah, and realize a brilliant dream of earthly domination. Hence the Jewish impostor sought popular support by personating a conquering Messiah. Had Jesus accepted the mission desired by his nation, Israel would have bestowed on him the crown of his father David. To imposture the temptation would have been irresistible. Yet Jesus turned from the dazzling reward. He chose thorns for his diadem, insults for acclamations, and a cross for a throne. Imposture never thus sets aside the tangible rewards of time for the invisible glories of eternity.

The agents chosen to establish and extend Christianity harmonized with its aims. Yet they were such as no human wisdom would select. What more absurd than the conversion of the world by obscure and unlettered men! Shall fishermen teach the doctors of Jerusalem, and overthrow the worship of the temple? Shall publicans instruct the philosophers of Greece, enlighten the wisdom of Egypt, and bring to their feet imperial Rome? Shall Johns and Peters and Matthews have place in that venerable succession which was illustrious with Moses the lawgiver, David the poet-king, Solomon the magnificent, and Isaiah and Jeremiah and Ezekiel, prophets splendid with genius, culture, and inspiration? Is the glory of a grand past to terminate in this vocation of men ignoble by birth and despicable by ignorance? A world changed from night to day and from death to life by such impotent instrumentalities! Nothing brought on Christ more ridicule and opposition than the choice of his instruments. Yet his wisdom was justified by his success. Fishermen and publicans have surpassed the lawgivers, the prophets, and the kings. Beyond Pentateuch and Psalter the glory of the Gospels! Patriarchs are dimmed by Apostles. Nor have the writings of the most brilliant Gentile genius the power of humble Jewish disciples. Plato and Aristotle and Virgil and Cicero, and all the other illustrious poets, orators, and philosophers of Greece and Rome, have never adorned by their works as many libraries, and been expounded in as many universities, and occupied as many transcribers and presses, and been read and proclaimed, like the Evangelists. Unlettered Apostles have become the teachers of our world. The impress of their writings is unrivaled. Not only have they regenerated nations, but created literatures, stimulated science, enlarged and beautified art, and collected around themselves the erudition of the ages. Mistake in the choice of agents would have made the triumph of Christianity impossible and proved Jesus an impostor. His selection was original and seemingly absurd. Yet by its magnificent success it vindicates his title to Messiahship.

Nor should we overlook the form of the Evangelical Histories. Had they been theological treatises, we can conceive their doom. Proverbially dry the discourses of divines! As graves hide deathheads and skeletons, so libraries entomb the mediæval theologians. Their treasures are known only to a few scholars. Over the multitude they have no power. Never could they convert mankind. Developed as theological systems, the Gospels would have been consigned to the shelf, and added to the dust of libraries. Drama and romance pass to the opposite extreme. They seek popular favor in the variety and vivacity of dialogue. Yet all is for artistic effect. In the Gospels are no imaginary scenes and personages moving in paint and robe and mimicry beneath a theatrical glare. Nor do we perceive a trace of those literary arts which would excite attention by fascinations of style and plot and character. Speakers and actors are real men. Theology is vivified into biography. Wisdom to teach ages springs from the most casual circumstances and trivial incidents. A woman met at a well, a detected adulteress, a reclaimed Magdalen, a poor widow, a trembling paralytic, a crucified thief, furnish words and deeds to instruct forever. Small events in time become types and teachers for eternity. Yet all so natural and spontaneous that we fail to perceive the beautiful plan of an everlasting wisdom. Nothing like this in any literature! Art transcended is forgotten. That dialogue which is the ideal of drama, romance, and philosophy assumes a living power over ignorance and learning, over free and slave, over classes and masses, over nations and races, over humanity. A divine Messiah could have no record superior to the Gospels.

How complete the life of Jesus! In other men you see mistakes—something defective, something unfortunate, something regretted! In all human brightness, however dazzling, a spot! A picture of Raphael, a statue of Angelo, the poem of a Dante, you can conceive improved. No mortal ideal beyond another touch! Yet none would change the life of Jesus! From manger to cross, from tomb to sky, unalterable, inimitable. By himself Christ stands in his pure and simple glory. All we could expect of Messiah he unites in career and character. And he only! Self lost in benevolence! An atmosphere of heaven's holiness! Always moving beneath a halo of love! Forgiveness for those who mock with the taunt and pierce with thorn and nail and spear! Benevolence in death! Dignity in resurrection! Majesty in ascension! If clouds receive the person of Jesus, they do not obscure his example. Down through the ages he lives in pious hearts. He is the spring of the noblest affections. He is the object of the sublimest hopes. He is the ideal of the most exalted moral aspirations and the incentive of the most loving lives and deeds. In the visions of the good his image is crowned with light from heaven. Take Jesus from the world, and you turn it into gloom! Let him reign, and humanity realizes its dream of universal light, love, and joy! In his system and character are all the marks of a divine Messiah!

But Jesus false, how black the picture! And how inconceivable the consequences! No middle place for this Christ, so perfect in character and so matchless in career! If not from the Holy Ghost in the Virgin, his conception a lie! If angels did not sing at his birth, aid after temptation and amid agony, and watch at his tomb, narratives of their appearances falsehoods! If no divine voice at his baptism, his ministry of holiness opening with imposture! If no suffering mortals relieved by his touch and word, his miracles of love fabrications! If no power as King over Hades, his promise on the cross to the thief of Paradise a deception! If no resurrection and ascension, fraud carried over life into death itself! Such mars and blots and twists in Jesus we may pronounce impossible.

One characteristic marks false religions. The moral they sacrifice to the ceremonial. Murderous Achilles is a pious hero if he presents libations and offers hecatombs. Paris may keep Helen if he sacrifices to Venus. A temple to his god condones the avarice of Pygmalion. The smoke of altars, the beauty of shrines, the pomp of processions, the magnificence of gifts, hide the lust of the heart and the evil of the life. How many sins has man forgotten in the glitter of his ceremonies! The splendor of philosophy has concealed vice and crime. Only one system begins in CONSCIENCE. Rituals and visions with old prophets were nothing to rectitude. Where the life was impure the sacrifice was abomination. Christ pierced the soul. The look of lust was sin. Repentance is the first trumpet tone of Gospel. Each man shall be tested in the fire of judgment. Holiness was the aim of Jesus, and holiness is the detestation of imposture. The holiness of Christ is an indubitable signature of his Messiahship.

Human nature resents boastful assertion. Time discovers imposture and scatters stolen plumes. Yet after centuries Jesus has universal veneration. Nor is his humble claim an element of this wide and loving and glowing esteem. What philosopher, ancient or modern, ever described himself in the terms Jesus appropriates? While canvas and marble represent his majesty, while poetry celebrates in song and architecture builds temples for his worship, while humanity appreciates his matchless merit, no man ever claimed for himself power so transcendant, obedience so implicit, authority so overmastering. Jesus describes himself as coming from God, working for God, going to God. He commands the forces of the universe. He is King over Hades. He will wake from their graves all the dead of the world. He will in glory be the Judge of humanity. He will award eternal life and eternal death. He, born in a manger, nailed to a cross, buried in a grave, is not mocked, but reverenced while he asserts the prerogatives of Godhead. Let any other man claim the powers and titles of Jesus! He will be ridiculed as a fool, or branded as a blasphemer. What would hurl another from his pedestal exalts Jesus in human esteem. Deep in man seems some instinctive recognition of him as indeed monarch of creation. A powerful presumption of his divine Messiahship!

Incarnation is the characteristic truth of Christianity. Homer and Virgil in immortal verse sang Jupiter, Mars, and Mercury. Olympus was earth

above the clouds. Each classic god a deified man!
But the Creator of all in our flesh! The Omnipotent! The Omniscient! The Omnipresent! The
Everlasting! In our humanity by deeds and words
to exhibit Him who built the universe! I can judge
whether such an attempt be fraud or failure. Here
is the test of Christ! What of his birth? Guiding
star and angel song amid celestial glory befit Incarnate Godhead. Nor less suitable the cloud over the
baptism, and the voice of the Father. No angel's
pen could exceed the narrative of the temptation.
And the mountain sermon that begins the ministry!
Let a cherub fly down and improve it! Blind Bar-
timeus challenges heaven. The glory of the transfiguration! The agony of the garden! The death
of the cross! Resurrection and Ascension! No
seraph could sing these as recorded in the Gospels!
Matthew the publican and John the fisherman do
this! They could more easily make the universe!
No mortal genius could invent the life of Jesus and
write it as I find it in the Evangelists. Suppose
him on the throne of his universe! His human
career is a worthy introduction to his divine exaltation. Of all ever on our earth, in Jesus only everything comports with Jehovah. The life of the man
harmonizes with the glory of the God. Throne in
heaven will not be ashamed of manger and cross and
tomb on earth. Angels blush at the life below! It
may well be their song and glory forever! Of
themselves never could unlettered Jews compose a
biography thus fitting a human career into the uni-

versal and everlasting kingship of Incarnate Jehovah. Nor is it mere style! Evangelists have no
Attic grace. Their power is in that life which makes
earth the admiration of heaven. In the character
of Jesus centers the argument of Christianity. My
reason trusts him, and hence believes his Bible.

## XV

### PROOFS OF THE RESURRECTION

ONCE I stood on the Jura to see Mont Blanc. Forty miles away the monarch seemed rising from Lake Geneva. His sublime summit glittered in the sun. Each peak about him I have forgotten. But he, the mountain-king, will live in my memory forever. Only as they added to his glory did I feel interest in lake, or hill, or vale, or cloud, or snow, or sunshine. Earth and sky were servants of his majesty.

As Mont Blanc amid mountains the resurrection of Christ amid proofs! Subserving it, type and prophecy and probability—all other inferior arguments. In it they find their place and power. Resurrection proved is Christianity proved. Resurrection rejected is Christianity rejected. Resurrection believed is Christianity believed. Then our inquiry involves everlasting life.

The scriptural proof of the resurrection of Jesus is *testimony*. Now, testimony in our courts is the evidence of witnesses to facts perceived by the senses. The law inquires not what a man thinks, but what he sees and hears. The Bible, then, bases Christianity on the *senses*. Our Lord appealed to *eye* and *ear* and *finger*. He claims to have been *seen, heard, touched* after his resurrection. To prove himself no disembodied spirit he ate fish and honeycomb. To his disciples he said, "Handle me and see," and afterward to Thomas, "Reach hither thy finger and behold my hands, and reach hither thy hand, and thrust it into my side." How clear and emphatic these words! "Thus it behooved Christ to suffer, and to rise from the dead, and ye are *witnesses* of these things." The specific function of the apostolic office was *testimony* to a risen Saviour. When choice was made to fill the place of Judas it was said, "Wherefore of these men who have companied with us all the time that the Lord Jesus went in and out among us, from the baptism of John unto the same day that he was taken up from us must one be ordained to be a *witness* of his resurrection." And in his Pentecostal sermon Peter cried to the Jews, "This Jesus hath God raised up, whereof we all are *witnesses*." Also at the baptism of the Gentile Cornelius the same apostle said: "And we are *witnesses* of all things which he did both in the land of the Jews, and in Jerusalem; whom they slew and hanged on a tree: him God raised up the third day and showed him openly, not to all the people, but unto *witnesses* chosen before of God."

We will consider the *fact,* the *mode,* and the *truth* of the testimony to the resurrection of Jesus Christ.

The *fact.* Nothing can be more simple than the point involved in our inquiry. It relates alone to motion—but to motion of a special kind. Winds, waves, galvanism, animal exertion, a thousand external powers in nature may displace a human body. Yet not one proves life. Now, let a force *within* the man move finger, or limb, or lip, or tongue, or eyelid! *This* motion shows the man is not dead.

When the will determines the action of the bodily organs, then there is life. To walk, to lift, to talk, or see, or hear from an *inner* volition is certain evidence of vital force. Or select a single function. Let the man speak! Then the man lives. And this without regard to previous condition. He who talks is alive if he had been dead. To prove life after death is to prove voluntary motion. Nothing more is required of the witnesses of Jesus than to show that after crucifixion voluntary motion ceased, and that this voluntary motion was restored. When he walked and talked before death he was alive, and if he walked and talked after death, he was alive. We have thus a question of fact to be determined by eye and ear.

The *mode* of the testimony. Trial by jury enables the court to scrutinize the face and person and manner of the witness. Often a look, a tone, a gesture will reveal a character. The determination of the case may depend on some trifling incident which is a searchlight to human purpose. Yet many lawyers prefer to have the witnesses examined in a private office and the testimony submitted to the judge on deposition. He then has an opportunity in retirement to weigh the evidence and reach a deliberate conclusion. Justice is as surely attained in this way as in the more hurried and excitable appeal to a jury. The record contains in itself all that is necessary for truth.

We cannot have before us for examination the apostolic witnesses to the resurrection. But the

Gospels resemble a legal disposition. St. Matthew and St. John describe what they saw and heard while St. Mark and St. Luke composed their narratives after investigating the reports of others. In the Acts St. Paul is described as having heard the voice of Christ, and seen his glory not only after his resurrection, but after his ascension. It is affirmed that his Lord said to him: "I am Jesus whom thou persecutest. But rise, and stand upon thy feet: for I have appeared unto thee for this purpose, to make thee a minister and a *witness* both of these things which thou hast seen, and of those things in the which I will appear unto thee."

In the case of eyewitnesses like St. Matthew and St. John we have the incomparable advantage of individual experience and testimony. But in biographers like St. Mark and St. Luke, who gather materials from many observers, we secure the obvious benefit of numbers. Few narrations are based on both methods. Hence the Evangelical Histories, in their mode of record, combine all possible excellences. And while we have established their authenticity by tracing them to the writers whose names they bear, yet this is not essential to our argument. We propose to show that the Gospels and the Acts, *in themselves,* enable us to judge the reliability of their witnesses to the resurrection. The Evangelical Histories are self-evidencing. They stand to us in the relation of a deposition to a judge. By them alone we can prove the resurrection, and, as we have said, the resurrection proved is Christianity proved,

Our inquiries culminate. They are focused into an investigation of the *truth* of the testimony of the witnesses to the resurrection of Jesus Christ. After his death did they *see* him? Did they *hear* him? Did they *touch* him? Did they *behold* him ascend from earth into heaven? As the lawyers say, we have narrowed the issue to a question of fact. I affirm that the evangelical witnesses are credible

I. BECAUSE OF THE SIMPLICITY OF THEIR NARRATIVES.

In our age a style has arisen called sensational. A modern reporter exhibits it. The sale of his narrative is the key to his style. If he can avoid it, he will not color and distort truth, yet he will not hesitate to draw from his imagination where invention is more popular and profitable than fact. The style of the reporter is always suspicious, and he is reluctantly accepted in a court of justice.

Now let us turn to the Evangelical Histories! Passing out of a gate of a city, our Saviour is said to have met a youth on a bier carried to his grave. To his mother, a widow, Jesus addresses two words, "Weep not!" and to the son, in the original, four, translated into English, "Young man, I say unto thee, arise!" It is briefly added, "And he that was dead sat up, and he delivered him unto his mother." Closing the narrative is a short record of the effects on the spectators and country. Death turned to life! The grave disappointed! A mother bearing back to her home the son she had been following to his burial! Yet not a comment, not an apology, not an inference, not an exclamation!

Tempest and billow! What sublime powers in nature! If subdued by Omnipotence, how signal the event! And venerable the man controlling mighty forces of the universe! Represented as monarch of these, with the simple majesty of conscious power, in a tempest, on a midnight sea, our Saviour says, "Peace! be still!" As few and simple his words when he commands his friend from the grave. He cries, "Lazarus! come forth!" In every part of the Gospels you perceive this style. There is no other. No mark of the impostor who sells his fraud for gold! In no instance strain, or bombast, or exaggeration.

While I speak let the earth shake, the sun grow dark, the sky be gloom, the rocks rend, the graves yield forth their dead! On the third day after let the crucified man who had been the central figure amid these terrors come from his tomb! In recording such facts an honest witness might be betrayed into exaggeration. A sensationalist fabricating for gain or fame would break forth into artificial extravagances. In the Evangelical Histories three Greek words describe the shaking earth; three the rending rocks; three the opening graves; thirteen the portentous gloom.

Equally simple the evangelical witnesses when narrating the resurrection. And a few plain words record the majesty of the ascension.

Is this the manner of impostors who trade in lies?

Created intellect can conceive nothing more sublime than the events related. A man is nailed to a cross. He is taken down dead, enrobed, embalmed, interred. He bursts from his grave. He walks the earth. He rises into heaven. By these acts he claims to have proved himself Jehovah Incarnate, Creator of all, the Messiah, the Redeemer, the King of the universe. Yet the style of the record is an everlasting contrast to the labored and pompous words by which knaves would impose magnificent forgeries.

The evangelical witnesses are credible

II. BECAUSE OF THE HONESTY WITH WHICH THEY NARRATE THEIR FAULTS.

Deceivers make the best of themselves. They hide their errors, and magnify their virtues, and yet in tone and look betray what they would conceal. Lawyers understand this, and turn it to account in examinations of witnesses and arguments to juries. When on the stand a man admits his errors; when he brings himself out into the light regardless of his interests; when he has no sensitive shrinking from exposure, he gains confidence from judge and jury. He is pronounced an honest witness.

Marks of truthfulness are visible in the Old and New Testaments as in no other volume ever written.

Noah, builder of the ark, second head of the race, progenitor of the Messiah, is described as intoxicated. No veil is cast over the deceits of Abraham, father of the Jew and favorite of Jehovah. What

pictures of the lies and frauds of Jacob, who saw a
ladder of glory from earth to heaven! We are
told impatient anger kept from Canaan Moses in-
trusted with the rod and law of God. Exposed and
punished the adultery and murder by David, whose
inspired Psalms during all ages were to express the
worship of the Universal Church. On the same
vivid and faithful pages we have recorded the idolatry and the concubinage of Solomon, together with
prayers that brought into his temple the cloud of
the divine glory, and words of wisdom which are
parts of Holy Scripture.

Nor in the Evangelical Histories concealments of
ugly and damaging facts. The childishness, the
stupidities, the rivalries of the apostles are all in the
Gospels, yet with none of the cant of a mock humil-
ity. What a temptation to hide the sins and follies
of men on whose testimony was to turn everlasting
salvation, and whose writings were to guide through
holiness to heaven! Spare Peter! Peter, prince of
apostles! Peter, witness of the transfiguration, and
companion of the agony! Peter, to hold for Jews
and Gentiles the keys of the kingdom of heaven, and
whose Pentecostal sermon is to be followed by the
effusion of the Holy Ghost! Peter will discredit
Christianity! Cover the blasphemer! Conceal the
liar! Have no record of the traitor! His curses
and falsehoods and treachery will make infidels.
Over all those coward apostles fling a veil! Such
would have been the cry of a human policy. Better
the divine honesty of Scripture! Better to know

14

the truth! Better that confession which proves infallibly the uprightness of the apostolic witness of the resurrection on whose words were to depend everlasting life! When these men say that after his death and burial they saw and heard Jesus we believe their testimony.

Again the evangelical witnesses are credible
III. BECAUSE OF THE VARIETY AMID UNIFORMITY OF THEIR NARRATIVES.

Let five rogues manufacture a story to impose on a judge! The villains will betray themselves. Anxieties to avoid contradictions produce suspicious agreements. Hence the artifice which conceals likewise exposes. To lawyers dovetailed testimonies prove fraud. But with harmony in essentials and difference in accidentals we are sure of honesty. And this mark of truth distinguishes the records of the resurrection. When first read they produce an impression of artless and hopeless contradiction. But when we obtain the clew the facts fall into their natural order, one narrative sheds light on another, and the whole history is changed from confusion into beautiful and convincing and enduring harmony. It is thus we have gazed in bewilderment on a painted scene. Now we learn the design of the picture. Our eyes fix themselves on the central figure, and the inferior personages assume their true relations. Flashed into us is the conception of the artist, and to the puzzle of disappointment succeeds a boundless confidence and delight.

The Evangelical Histories are credible

## IV. Because they proved sincerity by sacrifice.

Martyrdom for a doctrine does not establish its truth. It only shows the honesty of the suffering witness. A man may burn for a bad cause as well as a good. But when he dies for a truth he proves that he believes it. Now, apostolic witnesses gave lives in testimony to one supreme fact. As a lens gathers sun rays to a point the Scriptures converge all their lines of light on the resurrection of Jesus Christ. This grand, sufficient, crowning proof depends on those *senses* the chemist employs when he analyzes a salt, the geologist employs when he examines a rock, the astronomer employs when he observes a star. Our witnesses died affirming they saw and heard and touched Jesus after his resurrection. To the visible, the audible, the tangible they gave evidence, and with their blood, before earth and heaven, sealed their testimony. Thus their sincerity is unimpeachable, while they witness, not to a philosophical opinion, not to a scientific speculation, not to a religious dogma, but to the plain, perceptible facts that Jesus arose from the dead and ascended into glory.

In his relation to the proofs of Christianity St. Paul stands by himself. His call and work were his own. Not only to Jesus risen, but to Jesus glorified, gives he witness. Yet to Jesus *perceptible by sense!* Although amid a celestial splendor outdazzling the sun, Paul testifies that he both *saw* and *heard* Jesus, who was therefore under terrestrial conditions making legal testimony possible.

Paul in another respect differed from the other apostles. They represented the world's toiling masses, while, by his birth, genius, and culture, he completed their common-sense testimony, and brought it into sympathy with the educated classes. We have the spectacle of a young Jew, brilliant in gift and promise, with the best Greek and Hebrew training, never, perhaps, surpassed in splendor and discipline of his powers, an intense Pharisee, commissioned by imperial Rome to bind and imprison Christians, near the city of his victims, blind and prostrate before an effulgence from heaven, testifying that he *saw* and *heard* the risen and ascended Jesus, and after a long life of toil and peril proving his sincerity by martyrdom.

Was Paul a deceiver for profit? Had he been a conscious liar, his character would have corrupted his writings. But in all these we have incontestable proof that from conversion to death he was a pure, true, honorable, self-sacrificing man. Besides, he could have no selfish interest in his change. Imposture never turns from wealth to poverty, from fame to shame, from courts to prison, from freedom to chains, from honors to the block.

Or was Paul deceived by his imagination? This, too, we must answer from his writings. Do these leave the impression that he was led through life to death by the phantom of a deceived sense and a disordered brain? His epistles, in all their parts, contradict the inference. They evince what admirable balance of mind! How full of practical wisdom! In no other compositions can we find rules so excellent for the formation of character and the guidance of life. Paul we can judge from his works. With an eloquence discreet, chaste, and beautiful he guards all domestic, social, and political relations. No fanatic with such power and reverence ever sanctified the marriage vow, and by teaching and example gave stability to government. Rome invades his country, seizes her capital, desecrates her temple, crucifies the Master of the apostle. Does he flame into rage and revenge like our modern anarchists who destroy with torch, dagger, and dynamite? No! As representing the lawful authority, Paul urges submission to Nero, the imperial monster from whom he was to receive his death stroke. Only the calm wisdom of a true soul ever achieved such a triumph over the vengeful passions of nature. I believe such a man when, through a life of labor, danger, and sacrifice, he testifies a fact witnessed by *eye* and *ear*. His memorable affirmation comes to me with the power of truth:

"For I delivered unto you first of all that which I also received, how that Christ died for our sins according to the Scriptures; and that he was buried, and that he rose again the third day according to the Scriptures: and that he was *seen* of Cephas, then of the twelve: after that, he was *seen* of above five hundred brethren at once; of whom the greater part remain unto this present, but some are fallen asleep. After that, he was *seen* of James; then of all the Apostles. And last of all he was *seen of me also*,"

Nor in our admiration of the brilliant gifts, the matchless epistles, and the splendid career of Paul must we underestimate the other apostolic witnesses. They were, indeed, plain men. But they had shrewd, strong sense, tried integrity, and a natural adaptation to their work. If in a momentary panic they proved cowards, they bravely and honestly confessed their weakness, and proved their steadfast courage by faithful lives crowned with constancy by martyrdom. And what writings have impressed our world like their Gospels? Slight the influence of Greek and Latin and English classics compared with that of the Evangelical Histories! Transcendent in power and success the apostolical witnesses! They could not be deceived in regard to Jesus Christ. Could they believe that through more than three years they saw him heal the sick, cure the deaf and dumb and halt and lame and blind, and beheld him, and handled him after his resurrection, when he never restored a palsied limb, never cleansed a leper, never relieved a suffering sense, never performed one miracle, never left his grave, never rose into heaven? Mistake was impossible!

Incredible that they were knaves! Reflect on the poison of imposture! How it pollutes and withers the moral nature! Vile souls make vile lives! If the apostolic witnesses forged falsehoods, they have inflicted on man the greatest wrong conceivable. And they could be no better than their deeds. Knaves preach repentance, conversion, holiness! Knaves proclaim the moral law! Knaves announce

universal judgment and everlasting retribution!
Knaves describe a holiness stainless as Jehovah!
Knaves exhibit lives of love, truth, and purity, die
martyrs, and by their acts and writings prove themselves the most successful moral regenerators of our
world! Only human credulity can accept such im-
possibilities in human nature.

But Jesus himself is the supreme witness to his
own resurrection. He claims to be God. Let us
see what this involves!

Modern Science boasts the extent and the accuracy
of her observations and conclusions. She shows a
universe under law. In regions infinitely distant
she discovers elements and combinations the same as
on our earth. Masses, too, she proves impelled by
the same force expressed in the same formula.
Mathematical exactitudes govern creation. If precision in the works, what in the Worker? Perfection in the force, the law, the effect, implies perfection in the Cause. Is Christ the Maker of the
universe? Then in Christ is the exactitude of the
universe. One mistake shows that he is not God!
From birth to ascension his life is exposed to my
scrutiny. His works! Are they worthy of Godhead? His words! Are they worthy of Godhead?
His character! Is it worthy of Godhead? His life!
His death! His resurrection! His ascension! Do
all comport with Godhead? He is represented as
rising to the throne of his universe encircled with
the glory of Godhead. Does his career on earth pre-
lude such an exaltation into heaven? I can answer

these questions. Before me in the Gospels are the words and the works of this Christ. Here are all the materials on which my reason can base a judgment. A claim to this divine ideal would prove any ordinary mortal an idiot or a lunatic. Christ alone of men bears the searchlight of truth. One error would brand him an impostor. No such error can I discover. He claims to be God, and his whole life supports his claim. In his parables inimitable beauty! In his discourses immortal power! In his deeds an overmastering benevolence! On his purity no spot! On his life no blemish! On his love no limit! Imposture create this ideal! Imposture shine in a moral beauty which is a model for men and angels! Imposture flash forth a glory of character ineffable as Godhead! Yet to this conclusion we are forced if Christ falsified in regard to his own resurrection! To discredit his testimony gives the lie to his life! You dethrone the ideal of virtue, and sink it beneath the level of the vilest conceivable knavery. Christ *predicted* his resurrection. Christ called himself *the* resurrection. Christ spoke *after* his resurrection. We have, indeed, to his resurrection the conclusive testimony of his own chosen witnesses. But above men, above angels, above his universe, is the word of Jesus himself, who, by conquering death, attests himself God and Creator of all.

# XVI

## NARRATIVES OF THE RESURRECTION

HENCEFORTH we will treat the resurrection as a proved fact. It remains to examine with care the narratives in which it is recorded. Truth gains by investigation; and especially stands forth with new power and vividness the grand crowning testimony to Christianity the more scrupulously we compare the Evangelical Histories. Critical examination gives certitude to faith.

The beauty of the words and deeds of Christ impart glow to the writers of the narratives of the resurrection. Plainly they were artless men kindled with the image of a Master who had exchanged a tomb for glory. Each wrote to record facts without reference to others. If this independent method resulted in seeming contradictions that have to be reconciled, it also prevents all suspicion of collusion among the evangelists. Having defended the integrity of the witnesses, we will now show the accuracy and the harmony of their narratives. Out of statements apparently confused and irreconcilable will be educed the order of a profound, consistent, and convincing wisdom.

Celestial messengers shine and speak amid the scenes of the resurrection.

1. St. Matthew records the appearance and address of *one* angel to the women.

2. In St. Mark we find "a young man sitting on the right side clothed in a long white garment."

An angel this in human form? His announcement is similar to that in St. Matthew. Both Gospels may relate the same event under different aspects so that there is no necessary contradiction.

3. St. Luke says that the women beheld "*two* men who stood by them in shining garments." The address, while similar in import, differs in form.

4. St. Matthew, St. Mark, and St. Luke include Mary Magdalene among the women at the sepulcher who saw and heard the celestial visitants. Yet in St. John scene, persons, words, incidents, widely differ from the accounts in the other three Gospels. There are "*two* angels in white sitting, the one at the head, and the other at the feet, where the body of Jesus had lain." Nothing is said by them about the resurrection or going into Galilee to meet the Saviour.

St. Matthew mentions only two women, "Mary Magdalene and the other Mary," as at the sepulcher. St. Mark adds Salome. St. Luke speaks of Joanna and "other women," while St. John names only Mary Magdalene.

To harmonize the evangelical records we must recall the events after the crucifixion. This, by friends and enemies, was regarded as the final test of the Messiahship of Jesus. All that he had wrought and taught was obscured in the shadow of his cross. None believed in a Christ slain ignominiously by Jew and Gentile. Over his cause was the gloom of despair. Joseph of Arimathea begged the body for burial, which was delivered to him by Pilate. The faithful disciple "wrapped it in a clean linen cloth, and laid it in his own new tomb, which he had hewn out in the rock: and he rolled a great stone to the door of the sepulcher, and departed." Priests and Pharisees request from Pilate a guard of soldiers. A watch is set. Until the morning of the third day there is no visible change about the tomb. At the dawn of the Sabbath the disciples begin to move toward the sepulcher. Some came impelled by their affections. Some were influenced by curiosity. Some brought embalming spices. In a few, perhaps, the promise of the resurrection had been revived amid the Sabbatic calm succeeding the terrible scenes of Calvary. The disciples differed in sex, in faith, in love, in zeal, in courage, in a thousand minute circumstances. Nor could they all have lived at the same distance from the sepulcher. Moved by different impulses, influenced by different motives, dwelling in different places, surrounded by different circumstances, they arrived at different times and in different companies.

Armed and remorseless Roman soldiers stand about the sepulcher. The shadows of the night still linger around the scene, and the place was amid the graves of the dead. Peril was in the approach. Nor had the blood and gloom and agony about the cross vanished from memory. Over all was a solemn mystery. The courageous would advance nearest the sepulcher, and anxious groups would stand gazing or conversing, with their souls in that awful place where centered the hope of humanity. Assisted by these suggestions, we can harmonize the narratives of the resurrection.

The sun has not yet risen over Olivet. In the glimmer of the twilight a group of women timidly approach the sepulcher with spices to embalm their Lord. Magdalene is there, and the other Mary. On their way Salome may have joined the company. They have been anticipated by an angel. Amid lightning and earthquake he has hurled to the ground the Roman soldiers, who have fled. The stone has been rolled away. The tomb is empty. The women are amazed and terrified. More bold than the rest, perhaps, Magdalene approaches first the sacred spot. But she flies in fear, and to the others brings the startling news.

While this happens, still lingering near the tomb, Salome and the other Mary see the celestial visitant. His raiment is white as snow, and his face dazzles like the lightning. He sits on the stone as a radiant and solitary guard over the deserted rock, and says in mortal speech with immortal lips: "Fear not ye: for I know that ye seek Jesus, which was crucified. He is not here: for he is risen, as he said. Come, see the place where the Lord lay. And go quickly, and tell his disciples that he is risen from the dead; and, behold, he goeth before you into Galilee; there shall ye see him."

Fleeing from the tomb, Magdalene met St. Peter and St. John, and told them the astounding facts. Amazed and affrighted, they run to see for themselves. Arriving first, St. John pauses reverently before the rock within which had reposed his Lord. Restrained by no such delicacy, with characteristic impetuosity St. Peter rushes by, passes through the door, stands within the sepulcher, and notes here the napkin which had bound the head of Jesus, and there the linen which had folded his person.

After the two apostles leave Magdalene returns to the tomb. She had not heard the celestial voice that cheered her companions. She is alone in her passionate grief. Not only is Jesus dead, but his body is gone. Her love cannot see it and embalm it. She stands in her solitary gloom, and then stoops and gazes into the sepulcher. Her loyal affection is rewarded. She beholds the radiancy of celestial watchers who brighten the place with their glory. Lo! "two angels in white, sitting, the one at the head, and the other at the feet, where the body of Jesus had lain." No monarch ever had such a guard at his grave. But angels cannot assuage that sorrow. Only Jesus brings joy to the desolate heart. Hark! A voice! The Master speaks to Magdalene, "Woman, why weepest thou?" "Because they have taken away my Lord, and I know not where they have laid him."

To woman angels first announced the resurrection. Alive after death, Jesus made himself visible first to woman. Woman is honored above apostles. And to woman reclaimed from degradation is the earliest appearance of the risen Redeemer! Exquisite the scene! "She, supposing him to be the gardener, saith unto him, Sir, if thou have borne him hence, tell me where thou hast laid him, and I will take him away. Jesus saith unto her, Mary." Her heart and lip reply, "Rabboni!" Thrilled and transported, Magdalene is too passionate and familiar amid her loving and adoring reverence. In all the wonderful scenes after the resurrection how earth and heaven meet and mingle! The terrestrial never lost in the dazzle of the celestial! The impetuosity of Peter! The reverence of John! The doubt of Thomas! The tear, the rush, the rapture of Magdalene! Jesus awes her with his gentle majesty! "Touch me not; for I am not yet ascended to my Father: but go to my brethren, and say unto them, I ascend unto my Father, and your Father; and to my God, and your God." He does not say, "Cowards, traitors, deserters, who fled and left me to my enemies and my agony!" How tender the words Jesus selects! My *brethren!* Of my dust and blood! Each, like myself, child of the Everlasting Father! We feel Jehovah's love breathing from the heart through the lips of Jesus. Passing from this tender interview, our Saviour comes to the other Mary and Salome. Equally affecting the sweetness and dignity of his words! "All hail!" he exclaims. The women prostrate themselves. They embrace his feet. They adore him as their Lord. But fear is in their worship. Jesus knows the trembling in those loving hearts. With sympathy in eye and tone he says, "Be not afraid: go tell my brethren that they go into Galilee, and there shall they see me."

Amid the events described Joanna and the other
Galilean women come on the scene. They are laden
with fragrant testimonials of affection. Behold
them at the sepulcher! Messengers from heaven
appear. "Two men stood by them in shining garments." Celestial light, emblem of love and hope
and joy, beams about all these angels as they move
amid our terrestrial gloom. Terrified by what
should have kindled rapture, the women fall on their
faces to the earth. They hear words of comfort
and rebuke: "Why seek ye the living among the
dead? He is not here, but is risen: remember how
he spake unto you when he was yet in Galilee, saying, The Son of man must be delivered into the
hands of sinful men, and be crucified, and the third
day rise again." Light flashes over those souls.
The Master's words grow bright in memory, and
turning from the sepulcher, "unto the eleven, and to
all the rest," the women tell the glad news of the resurrection.

St. Luke adds words which seem to include the
totality of these manifestations. "It was Mary
Magdalene, and Joanna, and Mary the mother of
James, and other women that were with them,
which told these things unto the apostles. And their
words seemed to them as idle tales, and they believed
them not."

Behold two disciples walking on their way to Emmaus! They have been conversing about the occur-
rences around the sepulcher, and especially the appearances of the angels to the women. Nor have

they been kindled into any glow of hope by the reported resurrection.  A third person joins these disappointed men, and as he talks their hearts burn with a new strange joy.  He refers to the prophets. He shows that the Christ was predicted to pass through suffering into glory.  He sheds light on the Scriptures.  Arrived at the village, he would press forward.  But burning with immortal love toward this stranger in mortal form, they constrain him to enter their abode.  "And it came to pass, as he sat at meat with them, he took bread, and blessed it, and brake, and gave to them.  And their eyes were opened, and they knew him; and he vanished out of their sight."  Kindled by his words, in the two disciples is a flame which must diffuse its glow.  They leave their village.  They return to Jerusalem.  They proclaim what they have heard with the assurance of joy.  "The Lord is risen indeed, and hath appeared to Simon.  And they told what things were done in the way, and how he was known of them in breaking of bread.  And as they thus spake, Jesus himself stood in the midst of them, and saith unto them, Peace be unto you."

The last three Gospels record this interview, each relating part of the Master's words.  St. Mark gives the first commission to preach and baptize.  St. Luke narrates the terror of the disciples and the memorable challenge: "Behold my hands and my feet, that it is I myself: handle me, and see; for a spirit hath not flesh and bones, as ye see me have." St. John informs us that coming into their midst and pronouncing the benediction of peace, Jesus, breathing on them, said, "Receive ye the Holy Ghost: whose sins ye remit, they shall be remitted; and whose sins ye retain, they shall be retained."

Thomas was not present at this interview. He doubted the testimony of the other disciples. To him the resurrection seemed an impossibility. The other witnesses were probably convinced without accepting the challenge of Jesus to prove his identity by touching his person. But Thomas has no scruples. He will examine the wounds of his Master. Nor is he rebuked as an irreverent skeptic. After eight days, when the doors were shut, Jesus stood in their midst with the blessing of peace and said to Thomas, "Reach hither thy finger, and behold my hands; and reach hither thy hand, and thrust it into my side; and be not faithless, but believing." "And Thomas answered and said unto him, My Lord and my God!"

Arranged thus, there is no conflict, but a beautiful harmony in the manifestations of Jesus after his resurrection.

In its affecting beauty incomparable the scene on the shore of Tiberias.

Morning glances over the sublime summits of Lebanon. As the dawn vanishes the shadows from the sun deepen from the eastern hills. Peter and John are in a vessel on the lake. What form on the land grows visible in the brightening light? The disciple who had been swifter on foot is now proved keener in eye. John exclaims, "It is the Lord!"

15

Impulsive Peter recognizes the face he loves. Girt
with his fisher's coat, he flings himself into the sea,
and swims to his Master. The others follow, and
soon all collect around a fire of coals. After dining,
words which will be memorable in heaven and re-
counted during eternity! Denying and blaspheming
Peter! What penitent coward ever had breathed
into him such a delicate and exquisite sympathy of
forgiving love! To picture the scene is impossible
to art. Nor can a word be omitted without marring
the effect. "Simon, son of Jonas, lovest thou me
more than these? He saith unto him, Yea, Lord;
thou knowest that I love thee. He saith unto him,
Feed my lambs. He saith to him again the second time, Simon, son of Jonas, lovest thou me?
He saith unto him, Yea, Lord; thou knowest that I
love thee. He saith unto him, Feed my sheep.
He saith unto him the third time, Simon, son of
Jonas, lovest thou me? Peter was grieved because
he said unto him the third time, Lovest thou me?
And he said unto him, Lord, thou knowest all
things; thou knowest that I love thee."

Farewell to earth for Christ is near. The world
he blasted in Eden has been the scene of his birth-
pangs, his life-sorrows, and his death-agonies, and
is soon to be exchanged for the crown of that kingdom where curse has become everlasting glory. All
the apostles stand together on a mountain in Galilee. Sublime pulpit for the last proclamation of
man's Redeemer! The wide earth, the free air, the
expanse of heaven, and the universal sun whose

beams bless all are symbolic of a commission extensive as our race and enduring as time. Omnipotence and Omniscience are in the words of Jesus. He associates himself in a Trinity with Godhead, and with the authority of Godhead impresses his final message: "All power is given unto me in heaven and in earth. Go ye therefore, and teach all nations, baptizing them in the name of the Father, and of the Son, and of the Holy Ghost: teaching them to observe all things whatsoever I have commanded you: and, lo, I am with you alway, even unto the end of the world."

On what spot shall Jesus say farewell to man? The place he chooses will live forever in the memory of heaven and earth. It will inspire the hearts of saints and the songs of angels. Fitly appointed is Olivet! The scene of cross and tomb should be overlooked by the mountain of ascension. And the earthly Jerusalem should brighten and linger in the eye of him who is to rise through clouds to the glory of that heavenly Jerusalem builded to be the seat of his throne and the metropolis of his universe. Nothing shall be wanting in that farewell. As Jesus exalts himself through the air to his crown he looks in love on the earth that pierced him. "He led them out as far as to Bethany, and he lifted up his hands, and blessed them. And it came to pass, while he blessed them, he was parted from them, and carried up into heaven."

Having thus shown the delicate and beautiful harmonies in the Evangelical Histories of the resurrection, I may be permitted a few comments on those narratives of facts so stupendous, so unexampled, and so impossible to human invention.

I. REMARK THE PROOFS THAT OUR LORD APPEARED IN HIS VERITABLE BODY.

Magdalene mistook Jesus for the gardener. He was therefore in his aspect a man. Recognition came through his familiar voice. This proves that after his resurrection he looked as before his resurrection. Salome and the other Mary embraced his feet because they knew him as their Lord. On his way to Emmaus his two disciples regarded him as an ordinary traveler until he broke bread and vanished out of their sight. But no cloud must obscure his identity. The proof of Christianity rests on the evidences of the resurrection. Hence Jesus asserted he was not a spirit, but had the flesh and bones of a veritable human body. Hence he ate meat and fish and honeycomb, showing by functions the most animalistic that he preserved his physical personality and was not sublimated into a specter beyond the legal proof by the senses. Hence his command to Thomas to feel his wounds and know by contact that he was the same Jesus who on the cross was pierced by nail and spear. By his flesh not healed he establishes his identity. On the shore of Tiberias the apostolic witnesses obey his voice made familiar by years of service, and casting their net, are rewarded by fishes. But already their risen Master had provided for his hunger. Spirits do not need fire and fish and bread. His food proves

the body of Jesus real and human. He was in our
flesh perceptible to sense. All these minute circumstances, so trivial and so incidental, were necessary to prove the identity of Jesus. Only on the
testimony of eye and ear and hand could the evangelical witnesses establish the resurrection and
place our immortality on an eternal foundation.

II. BUT THE BODY OF JESUS HAD ALSO,
AFTER HE CAME FROM THE TOMB, SUPERNATURAL
ATTRIBUTES.

During his ministry he lived like his disciples.
His witnesses thus acquired that familiarity with
his person which gave certitude to their testimony.
After his resurrection he did not mingle with men.
His appearances were casual, sudden, and extraor-
dinary. During his absences where did Jesus live?
Was his couch in cave or wilderness? Were angels
his companions? Did he dwell in solitude? What
supported his human life? Or, invisible, was he
yet present with his disciples? He could see, hear,
eat, walk, speak, but he also came unseen and vanished suddenly. When the doors were shut he entered, with the facility of a spirit, while yet having
the aspect and attributes of a man, and always pre-
serving that majesty suitable to a body inhabited
by Godhead.

III. IN THE ACT OF ASCENSION THE BODY OF JE-
SUS MUST HAVE BEEN TRANSFORMED INTO ITS
GLORY.

There is a law wider than death, or our world,
or our system. Gravitation rules the universe. Dur-

ing his earthly career the flesh of Jesus was subject
to earthly conditions. Suddenly on Olivet his mortal state is changed. No longer can he be held by
the force of gravitation. Some transformation ex-
empts him from physical law. Yet till concealed
by the cloud he is visible. And if perceptible by a
physical organ, he is not wholly a spiritual substance.
We need not speculate when he was changed into
that radiancy of everlasting splendor which dazzled
Paul and prostrated John, and is befitting the majesty of the monarch of the universe.

## XVII

### CONSEQUENCES OF THE RESURRECTION

NOTHING more promotes skepticism than forgetfulness of the resurrection as a proved fact and a living power. Testimony to its truth was the grand apostolic function. In it by lip and life each disciple must witness faith. Scattered through Old and New Testaments, over more than four thousand years of history, innumerable supernatural attestations confuse and overwhelm the mind. A pilot is not wise who steers by small perplexing hills when his course is made plain by one sublime mountain rising above clouds into sunlight. A solitary peak, Everest, dominates the Himalayas. It towers with monarch majesty, and is a landmark for millions. Like this mountain-king over India, so is the resurrection of Jesus conspicuous amid the evidences of Christianity. By it reason guides and certifies faith.

Let me now trace the consequences of the resurrection of Jesus Christ!

I. IT ESTABLISHES HIS DIVINE MESSIAHSHIP.

To the Samaritan woman at the well Jesus first confessed himself the Christ. He blessed Peter who called him Christ. To his judges he answered that he was the Christ. Amid his death-agonies Jews taunted him as Christ. The challenge of the cross was met when he came from the tomb, and out of Scripture proved himself the Christ. Had he not risen, the reproach of crucifixion would have annulled Messiahship. THIS resurrection established forever.

Jesus exerted the attributes and claimed the dignity and performed the acts of Godhead. He pardoned sin with the sovereignty of Godhead. He wrought miracles with the power of Godhead. While on the cross, shaking his earth and darkening his sun, he was reviled for his claim to Godhead. The reproach at his death he answered by his resurrection. He permitted Thomas to call him God. In his great commission he asserted Omnipotence, and implied Omniscience and Omnipresence, and placed himself in equality with Father and Spirit. But had he turned to decay in Joseph's tomb, then in Joseph's tomb had been buried his pretension. His resurrection proved his Godhead. To this, as to his Messiahship, his apostolic witnesses testified in sermon and epistle. The Apocalypse exhibits him worshiped as Creator and Redeemer by his universe, whose adoration establishes his Godhead.

Like the cloud at the Red Sea, prophecy had a dark and a bright aspect. Here its pictures black with the gloom of defeat and despair, and there glowing with joy and victory! In the lowly birth and painful life and humiliating death of Jesus was fulfilled the woe, and in his resurrection and ascension was fulfilled the triumph. Jews had expected a temporal Messiah with an earthly throne at Jerusalem. Jesus, as King of his universe, is lifted into heaven—a consummation beyond all Hebrew imagination, yet realizing the types and promises and predictions of ages! A divine Messiah on the cross, by the offering of himself making one atonement in blood for sin, threw back on the Old Testament and forward on the New an unsurpassable glory. The past was not cast aside as dead. It furnished to the sacrifice of Jesus a living language. It vivified Moses into a fresh, immortal beauty. It supplied from the Law apt and varied and exhaustless illustrations for the Gospel. In the divine Messiahship of Jesus old and new mingle and harmonize, and the whole Scripture is illuminated with an everlasting light.

II. THE RESURRECTION OF JESUS ESTABLISHES THE DIVINE AUTHORITY OF THE OLD TESTAMENT.

He quoted Scripture in his temptation. He said in his Sermon on the Mount that he came to fulfill Scripture. He appealed during his ministry to Scripture as the word of God, and recommended its search to the Jews. After his resurrection he resumes his use of Scripture: "Beginning at Moses and all the prophets, he expounded unto them in ALL the Scriptures the things concerning himself. Then opened he their understanding, that they might understand the Scriptures." ALL the Scriptures! Jesus received the WHOLE Scripture of his time then in the homes and schools and synagogues of his people. He, a Hebrew, approved and expounded Hebrew Scripture whose books compose our own Old Testament. In his passage from his grave to his throne he placed on it the seal of his divine Messiahship proved by his resurrection.

Tradition Jesus assailed. As corrupters of his nation, its teachers he denounced with a fire of indignant rebuke reserved, not for publicans, but Pharisees. Had Scripture erred, could he have been less faithful? Would he not have warned the Jew and condemned his rabbis? Was not this demanded of the Messiah? Jesus did the reverse! He witnessed himself by Scripture; he quoted Scripture as authority; he called Scripture God's word; he received and reverenced and recommended Scripture from his temptation to his ascension. He did not insinuate crudeness and mistake. Nor did he wrest from Moses the authorship of the Pentateuch, refer portions of it to an age a thousand years later, and make it contemptible by novel theories and minute criticisms changeful as their chameleon authors. He did not tell us that Proverbs is a legend, Ecclesiastes a philosophical enigma, Canticles an amorous epithalamium; that Daniel was a forgery after the events predicted, and the entire Old Testament a mixture of myths, puerilities, barbarisms, and indecencies. Nay! On the *whole* Hebrew canon the risen Messiah placed the imprint of his attested divinity. Then we must acknowledge his Godhead and submit to his sovereignty! Before his universe Jesus has assumed responsibility for the Old Testament. I believe that learning and argument are wholly with him. But besides learning and argument, my reason trusts him because it has *proved* his Messiahship and his Godhead.

Skeptical satirists have always met the Old Testament with ridicule. Wit pays and pleases, while argument is often sober and laborious. The populace loves fire-shows, and youth enjoys a laugh at the expense of wisdom. Hence the temptation to flings at Scripture by press and pulpit. But behind everything our times love truth and justice. To still a world's unrest is the Bible's aim. In manly proofs reason will find support for faith.

Our sensitive and refined moralists are offended with the alleged severities and immodesties of the Old Testament. Its defense is not difficult. But we need not attempt details. We have to all objections always one all-answering argument—it is the risen Christ. He proved incarnate truth; he proved personified holiness; he proved infinite love and wisdom has placed his sanction on the Old Testament. Are we purer and loftier than he? What he approves I accept.

He who rejects Moses questions Christ. Unpersuaded by Moses, men grope and falter about Christ. How express the words of Jesus? "If ye believe not Moses, ye will not believe me." Here Christ links himself to Moses. Christ and Moses stand and fall together. To stab Moses wounds Christ. What do hypercritics demand? That for theories forever spawning, forever warring, and forever changing I should set aside the opinions of rabbis and the traditions of the Jews; that I should abandon the best results of Christian scholarship and the final testimony of the Christian Church; that I should sacrifice all the evidences establishing the

Messiahship and Godhead of Jesus, and cast away his own solemn and repeated approvals, before and after his resurrection, of the Old Testament as the foundation of the New. All my sunlight of proof I must obscure by a mote of criticism. My faith, then, must be fickle as fashions of human opinions. It is to shift like the winds, vary like the tides, veer like the whims of mortals. I am left a rudderless ship on a midnight sea. Abandoning my reason and my faith, I am directed to build my house on ocean billows. Never! By invincible argument I have proved Christ risen from the dead. That true, all opposed is false. The Messiah is the attested Incarnate God! I, then, must trust his word. Because he approves the Old Testament I approve the Old Testament. Reason rests my faith, not on mist, but rock—HIMSELF.

III. THE RESURRECTION OF JESUS ESTABLISHES THE DIVINE AUTHORITY OF THE NEW TESTAMENT.

The integrity of the apostolic witnesses has been proved. Testimony to their risen Lord was their supreme vocation. Accepted for his resurrection, they will be accepted for his teaching. If we believe them for fact, we must believe them for doctrine. Turn to the words of Jesus! Borrowed from the old, they illuminate the new. Types of Moses are illustrations with Christ. Pass from Gospels to epistles! Germs of the Master in his servants expand into flower and fruit. In the Gospels Jesus speaks with the authority of a lawgiver proclaiming his sovereign will. His meaning needs exposition by his authorized commentators. The statute of heaven must be intelligible to earth. Epistles explain Gospels. But Gospels and Epistles teach the same doctrine! Is doctrine the same? So are writers! All the Gospels are under the seal of apostolic witnesses to the resurrection, and all the Epistles are under the seal of apostolic witnesses to the resurrection. Hence all bear together the stamp of the resurrection. The apostolic witnesses to the facts of the Gospels become, in the Epistles, apostolic witnesses to the doctrines of the Gospels. And Gospels and Epistles thus alike refer back for authority to the risen Christ.

Inspired by God, we may presume that the Bible will be preserved by God. He would not dictate truth, and then let it fail to accomplish his purpose. This neglect would defeat himself. Having made the record, he will guard the record. But as to the epistles, we are not left to inference. For their writers Jesus supplicated unity from the Father and promised the Spirit of the Father. Also for their work they received his baptism of light. Jesus, in advance, became security for unity and truth in the epistles of his apostolic witnesses. The New Testament is thus one system announcing and expounding the will of the risen and ascended Redeemer.

During his ministry the apostolic witnesses were companions of their Lord. They lived under his eye and were taught by his lips. As they received his instruction, so they were enlightened by his Spirit. Their gifts were inalienable, intransmissible, inestimable. In the Apocalypse they are throned and crowned around their King. Afterward their names were in the foundations of his celestial metropolis. Written by them, the New Testament has an unapproachable sanctity and authority. On their testimony we receive the life everlasting. Matthew! John! Peter! Paul! They are not on the human level of Augustine and Luther and Calvin and Cranmer and Wesley. Apostolic witnesses and writers are no common stones in the temple of our salvation. They are pillars of the edifice built on our incarnate risen and glorified Messiah.

When by death of the apostles ended the possibility of addition to the New Testament inquiries commenced about the canon. This we know from Fathers and catalogues and commentaries. During centuries several epistles were questioned and discussed. The Apocalypse was held longest in suspense, and omitted even by the Council of Laodicea. Genius and learning exhausted all their resources to attain truth. Both Greek and Latin Churches finally received as canonical all the books we find in our own English Bibles. The whole past of the world was upheaved by the Reformation. Luther cast aside pope and tradition and Apocrypha, and appealed to Scripture as the sole standard of inspired and authoritative truth. But he was forced to meet the question, What is Scripture? The test of Luther overthrew the very principle of the Reformation he had created, and unsettled the foundations

of the Scripture on which he built his edifice. He
rejected whatever did not teach or imply justifica-
tion by faith. St. James he eliminated, and cast
ridicule on St. Paul in Galatians. The canon was
to be determined, not by the pope, but by Doctor
Luther. Nor was Zwingle less dangerous. He
banished from Scripture all that, in his view, did
not promote God's glory. Germany and Switzer-
land seemed combining to confuse those truths which
had shaken the pope and were to reform the world.
Calvin saw the peril. His foresight of genius rescued Christianity from its abyss. By his efforts
was secured the Protestant acceptance of the canon
as found in our Anglican Bible. We are no longer
left to the feelings and prejudices and preferences
of sects and individuals in determining what is
authoritative Scripture. That external sanction
Christians desire, and think wanting, we possess.
On certain books the consensus is universal. About
patriarch and pope and tradition and Apocrypha
communions differ. But in regard to the books
in our Anglican Bibles all agree. Every book
is accepted by the Greek Church. Every book is
accepted by the Latin Church. Every book is
accepted by the English Church. Every book is
accepted by the Protestant Communions. For our
own Old and New Testaments we have the voice of
Christendom. Here is the promise of its unity. It
has one universal standard which will assimilate the
world to itself. However different the parts of the
superstructure of Christianity, its temple rests on

the everlasting foundation of the same Holy Scripture. Through stormy centuries Almighty God has guided to this result. For our Bibles we have not the clouded and changeful sanction of individual judgment and subjective impression and variable emotion. We have the authority of Christendom—an external authority, and the highest conceivable or possible—an authority involving the gifts of piety and genius and erudition during ages; not the result of hasty and superficial investigation, but of the learned and patient labor of centuries—an authority above priests, bishops, popes, and patriarchs—an authority beyond particular communions and general councils; yet not an authority against these, but including these—an authority embracing laity and clergy, and Church Universal—an authority, therefore, Greek and Latin and Protestant—supreme, catholic, indestructible—speaking to all regions and generations, and proclaiming to earth and heaven that our Lord, attested Messiah by his resurrection, places on the whole Bible, Old Testament and New, the seal of the truth, power, and majesty of his Everlasting Godhead.

FINIS.